Library
St. Marys High School
St. Marys, Pa

LOBBYING

LOBBYING

KAREN SAGSTETTER

American Government Series

Consulting Editor, Richard Darilek

Department of History
Herbert H. Lehman College
The City University of New York

Franklin Watts
New York | London | 1978

Cartoons courtesy of:
Frank Baginski: p. 2;
ROTHCO: (Graham-Arkansas Gazette) pp. 9, 61, 78;
(Bender-Waterloo Courier) p. 20; (Renault-McClatchy
Newspapers) pp. 31, 73; (Liederman-L.I. Press) p. 43;
(Whitman-Phoenix Gazette) p. 56; (Fink) p. 65;
(Valtman-Hartford Times) pp. 85, 88, 94;
(Pearson-Knickerbocker News) p. 99.

Poster courtesy of Common Cause: p. 68.

Library of Congress Cataloging in Publication Data

Sagstetter, Karen.
    Lobbying.

    (American Government series)
    Bibliography: p.
    Includes index.
    SUMMARY: Discusses the history, function,
and current actions of lobbying and lobbyists in the
United States.
    1. Lobbying—United States—Juvenile literature. [1. Lobbying] I. Title.
JK118.S28   328.73'07'8   77-12302
ISBN 0-531-01413-4

19,364

Copyright © 1978 by Franklin Watts, Inc.
All rights reserved
Printed in the United States of America
5 4 3 2 1

For Randy, Brad, and Leigh
my brothers

ACKNOWLEDGMENTS

My thanks to:

Richard Darilek and Jane Steltenpohl for the opportunity to write this book and for intelligent criticism and editing which vastly improved the manuscript.

Stanley Rubin and Robin Roy Rubin, Jarold Ramsey, Loretta Marion, Wendy Atwell, Judy Hill, Lois Markham, Lee Schwarz, Virginia Lloyd-Davies, and David Sisson for friendship and encouragement at crucial times.

Peter R. Lloyd-Davies, my husband, for everything.

CONTENTS

CHAPTER ONE
Lobbying: An Historical Overview 1

CHAPTER TWO
The Modern Lobbyist at Work 19

CHAPTER THREE
Lobbying in Action: The National Rifle
Association vs. Gun Control 39

CHAPTER FOUR
In Search of the Public Interest 55

CHAPTER FIVE
Regulating Lobbying 77

FOOTNOTES 101
BIBLIOGRAPHY 105
INDEX 107

LOBBYING

CHAPTER ONE

Lobbying: An Historical Overview

Lobbyists are people dedicated to persuasion. They labor in city council rooms, state capitols, and federal halls. Whenever and wherever government operates, lobbyists are working to influence policy. But the exact nature of the lobbyist's job remains a mystery to most of us. Who is a lobbyist? What exactly is lobbying? Who hires lobbyists? Are they ethical, or slightly outside the law? And, most important of all, how does lobbying fit into our current system of government?

A lobbyist is someone who tries to influence legislation or government policy. Such a person usually represents a special or public interest group. Occasionally, someone lobbies on his or her own behalf. Here is an example of lobbying in action:

A man from Montana walks into a House Office Building in Washington, D.C. He has an appointment with his Congressman. His speech is brief and to the point. "Hello, Congressman Kong," he says. "I'm a lobbyist for the United Fly Catchers, and we want

"No, I am not an anti-lobbyist!"

to encourage you to vote against the proposed bill that would restrict fly catching in the western states. We believe fly catching is vital to the national interest for ecological reasons and as a check against the spread of sleeping sickness."

Congressman Kong scratches his belly and promises the lobbyist he'll consider the United Fly Catchers' point of view.

Later that day, a staff member from the Department of the Interior visits Congressman Kong. Interior is a division of the executive branch of the federal government. It is chiefly concerned with natural resources. It is this department that will see that the fly catchers' bill is carried out if it becomes law. Three lunchtime meetings have been held concerning the bill. The staff member has come to inform Congressman Kong of the discussions.

"Congressman Kong," she says, "we in the Department of the Interior, after consulting with the President, believe that you should vote *for* the fly catching bill. The President believes that flies are fast becoming an endangered species. He'd like to see the United Fly Catchers forced to lay off the fly population."

Congressman Kong again scratches his belly and promises the lobbyist he'll consider her point of view.

This is lobbying, and it goes on continually wherever there is government. Different branches of government try to influence each other, as in the case of Interior's visit to Congressman Kong. Representatives from state governments lobby Congress to vote them highways. Local interests lobby city governments for sewers or new schools. Foreign countries employ lobbyists to argue about tariffs or defense agreements before Congress and the President. Private corporations and citizens' groups use lobbyists to petition Congress and the executive branch to uphold their rights as guaranteed by the United States Constitution. In fact, the First Amendment *forbids* the federal government to make any law limiting freedom to petition (and, therefore, lobby) the government.

But the government requires lobbyists to identify themselves. From the *1975 Directory of Registered Lobbyists and Lobbyist Legislation* we can get an idea of just how much lobbying activity goes on. Listed are such groups as the Distilled Spirits Institute, the United States Cane Sugar Refiners' Association, the Southwestern Peanut Shellers Association, the Japanese-American Citizens League, the National Student Association–Government and You, Common Cause, the American Camping Association, the Coca-Cola Company, the American Association of Retired Persons, the American Society of Composers, Authors, and Publishers, the National Federation of the Blind, and Antelope Airlines.

As of 1975 more than 1,500 people were registered as lobbyists in the District of Columbia, about three times as many lobbyists as there were members of Congress! However, because of a loophole in the law that will be discussed later, many lobbyists do not register. It is estimated that there are thousands of lobbyists working to influence legislation at the federal level, and many more work at the city, county, and state levels.

PRIVATE VERSUS PUBLIC INTEREST

Lobbyists are representatives just as members of Congress are representatives, but lobbyists are not elected. They generally represent an *interest* or an *interest group*. An interest group is made up of those people united in support of policies or ideas that are important to its members. Such groups often hire professional lobbyists to argue their cases before city, county, and state governments, Congress, the federal government, or the various agencies of the federal government. Generally speaking, a private interest promotes policies that benefit its members. Its interests are usually special or narrow. In contrast, the "public interest" represents the needs and desires of the majority of citizens. Thus, the policies that presumably benefit the public and are not aimed at protecting or supporting a special group are said to be "in the public interest." Many lobbying groups have recently sprung up to promote such policies.

For example, suppose there is a law requiring unit pricing on food products. The law is designed to help consumers compare prices more easily. In unit pricing, product labels explain the price per quart, pound, and so on, of each item. If Letty's Tuna Fish costs thirty-five cents a can and weighs six ounces, and Coral Reef Tuna costs forty-three cents for a seven-and-a-half-ounce can, it is difficult to figure out which one is cheaper *per ounce*. Since everybody buys groceries, a law requiring unit pricing is considered by some citizens' groups to be in the public interest.

On the other hand, a law that taxes imports on chocolate is likely to protect domestic candy manufacturers from foreign competition. Such a law would most likely not be in the public interest. Suppose that Maybury Bars are produced in Holland and sold in the U.S. for twenty-five cents. A similar American candy bar, Zounds, costs thirty-five cents. As a consumer, you may prefer the cheaper chocolate. However, Zounds lobbies for a tax on Maybury Bars. The tax will increase the price of a Maybury Bar to fifty cents. Now you'll be more likely to buy Zounds Bars because they're only thirty-five cents. Zounds represents a *private* interest, because it is the only group that benefits from the policy it is pushing.

Lobbies that speak for the public may be financed by many different groups. On the other hand, a private interest group usually speaks only for the people who support it financially, or who work in that particular industry. The candy lobby isn't likely to petition the government on behalf of the wheat growers. One woman has been pressuring Congress for years to use the corn tassel as the national floral emblem. She represents a *very* private interest.

Lately it's become common for lobbyists to claim their favored policy will contribute to the public good, whether it will or not.

Government officials like our Congressman Kong must in the end sort out the conflicting claims and decide for themselves how to vote.

THE SCOPE OF LOBBYING

Intense lobbying takes place whenever a bill before Congress is controversial, may cost the taxpayer a lot of money, or will probably affect many people. Lobbying activity also increases dramatically when issues affect important industries, unions, or citizens' groups. Some of the issues argued by lobbyists and lawmakers in the sixties and seventies were the Vietnam War, Middle East relations, no-fault insurance, traffic safety, campaign financing, the Alaskan pipeline, gun control, busing, dairy prices, and the impeachment of President Nixon.

From 1969 to 1973, for example, debate over whether or not a pipeline should be built to carry oil across Alaska resulted in a major lobbying battle. Favoring the pipeline was the Alyeska Pipeline Service Company, which was to build and run the pipeline. This company was formed by seven major oil companies, including Exxon, Mobil, and Arco, a subsidiary of Atlantic Richfield. Other supporters of the pipeline were the American Petroleum Institute, the American Gas Association, the state of Alaska, the Alaska Federation of Natives, and the Alaska Association of General Contractors. Opponents, who collectively called themselves the Alaska Public Interest Coalition, included Common Cause, Consumer Federation of America, Friends of the Earth, National Wildlife Federation, the Sierra Club, Trout Unlimited, and the United Auto Workers. Congress eventually decided to go ahead with construction of the pipeline. This was considered a major victory by pro-pipeline lobbyists.

Nearly every voter is represented indirectly by a lobbyist at some time or other. A citizen who favors no-fault insurance, for example, has that interest represented by lobbyists, even though he or she didn't personally do anything about it. For example, in 1976, the National Association of Manufacturers (N.A.M.) had about 13,000 active members, companies engaged directly in manufacturing. The United States Chamber of Commerce is both a business and a professional federation. In 1976 it had more than 4,000 organization members (state and local chambers of commerce and trade associations), plus over 40,000 business members (individual companies and businesspeople). Both the N.A.M. and the Chamber of Commerce lobby extensively on issues related to business. In fact, most of the work done by the Chamber's national office is related to influencing government. The number of voters indirectly represented by the N.A.M. and Chamber of Commerce must number in the hundreds of thousands.

One measure of a lobby's power is the amount of money it spends. In 1973, organizations reported spending $9.7 million to influence government decisions. This information was disclosed because of the Federal Regulation of Lobbying Act. However, it is only part of the money actually spent. Loopholes in the law allow groups to avoid releasing spending reports.

In 1973, the top spender was Common Cause, known as a citizens' lobby, which reported $934,835. It was followed by the United Auto Workers with $460,992, and the American Postal Workers Union with $393,399. Other leading spenders were the American Federation of Labor–Congress of Industrial Organizations (AFL-CIO), American Trucking Association, Inc., American Nurses Association, Inc., U.S. Savings and Loan League, the Gas Supply Committee, and the Disabled American Veterans.

Much of the money *not* reported because of loopholes in the law was spent by pressure groups trying to influence various federal executive agencies. These agencies are set up to enforce the laws made by Congress. For example, the Interstate Commerce Commission (ICC) oversees the transportation industry; the Federal

Communications Commission (FCC) oversees the communications industry, and so on. Accordingly, lobbyists are regularly employed to influence executive department decisions. Thus, when the trucking industry wants a rate increase, trucking lobbyists spend much time and money to persuade the ICC to go along with them.

Lobbying of legislators, executive departments, and courts takes place on all governmental levels—local, state, and federal. The result is a tremendous impact on the processes of government. Lobbyists are every bit as important in shaping our government policies as elected representatives.

LOBBYING BY FOREIGN GOVERNMENTS

Foreign governments also try to influence American legislators when a policy that affects them is being considered during treaty negotiations for example, and debates on foreign aid or defense policies. A recent incident involved the South Korean government. Apparently, the government of Park Chung Hee became concerned during a seven-month fight in Congress in 1969–70. The debate centered on an additional $50 million in military aid to South Korea. The South Korea lobby, consisting of Korean businessmen and government officials, began an effort to influence U.S. politics. Among other things, they hoped to persuade the U.S. Congress to increase aid to South Korea during a time of public disenchantment with aid to Asia. In late 1976, several members of the House of Representatives admitted receiving money as gifts or contributions from Korean sources. As with other kinds of lobbying, efforts by foreign governments to influence legislators are permissible as long as the activity is conducted openly.

The Foreign Agents Registration Act of 1938 requires that agents of foreign governments must properly register with the Attorney General and must disclose lobbying activities. Members of Congress are also subject to regulation under the law. The problem in the Korean case is that many of the lobbyists did not regis-

ter. The Korean lobby is now being investigated by the Justice Department and the House Ethics Committee. However, legitimate lobbying by foreign governments is quite common. Their interest in influencing U.S. policy results in lobbying efforts similar to those engaged in by American interest groups.

THE PRESIDENT'S LOBBY

When the staff member from the Department of the Interior visits Congressman Kong, she is lobbying in a way that has become especially significant since World War II; this lobbying is how the executive branch of government, led by the President, influences Congress. Many claim such influence is as important as interest group pressure.

The President and the executive departments, such as Interior, Health, Education, and Welfare, Commerce, and Defense, have grown more and more powerful since World War II. Depression, war, and postwar international politics caused President Franklin D. Roosevelt and his successors to propose a variety of new laws and programs. These proposals needed selling to Congress. Thus, lobbyists became a regular part of the President's staff. Roosevelt's assistants met often with members of Congress. They would present drafts of bills and argue for passage. Though the crisis period passed, this type of lobbying continued. Former President Richard Nixon employed a sizable staff to work with Congress. The head of that group began his day at 7:30 A.M. with meetings concerning the status of bills in which the President was interested. He would then do reports and memos, write letters, and make an estimated 125 phone calls a day. Almost all this activity related to convincing lawmakers to go along with the executive branch's programs. Each department, in addition, has its own lobbyists. This steady pressure results in "special interest" lobbying, like that engaged in by private lobbies.

Public and private interests, intergovernmental influence, in fact, all the lobbying taking place in this country today adds up to an enormous industry. Let's look now at how lobbies began and developed into today's "fourth branch" of government.

THE HISTORY OF LOBBYING

In Argentina, the word *lobbear* is slang for sitting around in hotel lobbies and eyeing the guests. The word "lobby-sitting" has sometimes been used in the same way in the United States.[1]

However, our present word lobby apparently derived from the medieval Latin word *lobium*, a covered walk or cloister in a monastery. It was first used in English around the middle of the sixteenth century. When the British parliamentary system developed, the word referred to the halls and corridors of the House of Commons.[2]

Our word *lobbying* comes from the fact (still often true) that the easiest way to get hold of legislators was to physically confront them in lobbies. So a lobbyist, or what the British call a lobby-agent, was someone who waited in the halls of legislative houses and grabbed lawmakers as they went by.

If a lobbyist is anyone who tries to influence government, then the tradition is very old indeed. Merchants who hung around kings and courts throughout history trying to gain favors certainly qualify as lobbyists. When a foreign ambassador hovered around the king looking for a favorable treaty, he was lobbying.

For Americans, lobbying comes directly from the right of petition. This right was claimed in the British portion of the New World at least as early as 1619. At that time the Virginia Congress, known as the House of Burgesses, claimed the right to petition the British Parliament on behalf of its people. In fact, many colonial assemblies came to see themselves as caretakers of popular rights.[3] If a colonist wanted to ask the British Parliament for something—a favorable tax, for example—his best bet was probably to do it through the colonial assembly.

The right of petition was thus part of the Declaration of Independence and was later included in the First Amendment to the Constitution. It is a liberty Americans have valued for a very long time. But unfortunately, it has also often been used as a means of gaining special or excessive privilege from government. Sometimes lobbyist pressure on officials takes the form of outright bribery.

In the history of Georgia, there is a case in point. Georgia had been having problems with its western lands. In 1795 the state decided to sell some of its holdings to land speculators. (Speculators are people who try to make money by reselling land for more than they paid for it.) These speculators pressured legislators to accept one cent per acre. They bribed the lawmakers with slaves, barrels of rice, money, and land. One man was offered 75,000 acres. Sure enough, a bill authorizing the transaction was introduced in the state assembly. The bill passed. But after it was signed by the governor, the people woke up. One legislator was driven out of the state. At the next election, the entire legislature was kicked out by the voters! The people were so outraged that they burned the bill at a public ceremony, erased all references to it from the state records, and passed a law setting a $1,000 fine for any future legislator who even mentioned the bill.

However, despite these rather extraordinary efforts, lobbying as a practice was there to stay, and by 1877 it had been so misused in Georgia that the voters declared it to be a crime. Lobbying in Georgia remained illegal until 1945.[4]

JAMES MADISON AND THE *FEDERALIST PAPERS*

Early lobbying in the U.S. was, of course, not confined to Georgia. Wealthy merchants were forever seeking special favors from the First Continental Congress. The potential dangers of lobbying were quite clear to the men who wrote our Constitution. It is all too human for an individual or small group to desire special consideration from the government, and to use slightly or grossly inappropriate means to get it. It is equally human for a legislator to yield to temptation. Throughout our history the question has come up again and again: What should be the proper balance between private and public interests? It was a question very much on the minds of men such as Thomas Jefferson, Alexander Hamilton, and James Madison.

In the late 1780s, the men who wrote the Constitution were trying to persuade voters to approve it. As part of their campaign, a series of eighty-five letters were published in New York City newspapers. They were written under the pseudonymn of Publius. Though the letters began to appear on October 27, 1787, it was some years before the identity of the authors, John Jay, James Madison, and Alexander Hamilton, became generally known. These letters are known today as the *Federalist Papers*. They represent some of the clearest analyses of constitutional government ever written.

In one of the *Federalist Papers*, James Madison discusses private or special interests (what he calls *factions*), and how they relate to the public interest. He says that "the public good is disregarded in the conflicts of rival parties," and warns against the "violence of faction." He defines a faction as a number of citizens "who are united and actuated by some common impulse of passion or of interest, *adverse* [author's emphasis] to the rights of other citizens, or to the permanent and aggregate interests of the community." That is, when a faction forms, it inherently goes against the public interest.

Madison believed, however, that the formation of factions is natural, rooted in our need to band together, like the need to eat, love, or work. People often differ on political, economic, social, and religious issues. But they enjoy joining groups of likeminded citizens. He also believed that the most vigorous disputes arise over the distribution of property, and that the most powerful faction will win out. Suppose you own a house in a neighborhood where a highway is scheduled to be built. You may sympathize with the commuters who want a new route into town. But you don't particularly want your own house torn down to make room for it. Who prevails? Who *should* prevail? These questions are very difficult to answer. They are usually confronted during the process of lobbying, as pressures are exerted by the most powerful interest groups or factions.

Madison thought that removing the source of the mischief—people's tendency to have a variety of viewpoints—was not only impossible, but undesirable. The result would be a country full of zombies—everyone having the same opinions. The right to split off into groups is a part of our freedom of expression. He concluded that "the causes of faction cannot be removed and that relief is only to be found in controlling its effects." He recommended a strong Union to counteract the effects of undesirable local factions. But in the nineteenth century, disputes between the competing interest groups or factions got out of hand. The wielding of power by a small group of industrialists far surpassed Madison's predictions.

THE NINETEENTH CENTURY

In the nineteenth century, U.S. industry grew quite rapidly. As manufactured goods, factories, and railroads multiplied, so did organizations and lobbyists—to see that the new industries were protected. Around 1825, Fredrich List, a German immigrant who worked as propagandist for a trade association, proposed that "the friends of domestic industry should meet annually to prepare the necessary legislation for Congress after discussing the measures and gathering the facts." [5] His idea was eventually put into effect. Business and labor organizations now prepare legislative programs each year.

By 1852, lobbying had increased so much that President James Buchanan wrote: "The host of contractors, speculators, stockjobbers [persons selling worthless securities], and lobby members which haunt the halls of Congress, all desirous . . . to get their arm into the public treasury, are sufficient to alarm every friend of his country. Their progress must be arrested." [6]

What exactly was going on? Some honest petitioning, but also some less respectable forms of persuasion such as bribery and manipulation. Thurlow Weed in the 1850s, for instance, displayed great skill in blending politics, business, and lobbying. His talent as an organizer together with strong leadership abilities made him one of the most influential men in politics, both in Washington and in Albany, the capital of New York. He became known variously as "the wizard of the lobby," the "Lucifer of the lobby," "father of the lobby," and "the dictator."

Weed had begun his career as a printer, then went to Albany, became the editor of the *Evening Journal*, and eventually got himself elected to the state legislature. During the 1830s and 40s he wrote many editorials advocating extension of voting rights and an end to slavery. He even warned against government financing of private interests.

Somewhere along the way, Weed lost his zeal for reform and became an agent for the same interests he had opposed in his editorials. James Deakin, in his book *The Lobbyists*, describes Weed's wheeling and dealing:

> When the Bay State Mills of Lawrence, Mass., decided to spend $70,000 in an effort to lower the duties on wool, $5,000 went to Weed through an intermediary, John W. Wolcott, a professional lobbyist. . . . Erastus Corning, president of the New York Central Railroad, got Weed to help him in seeking extra compensation from Congress for a construction company in which Corning was interested.

Some letters to Weed are revealing. For example, A. S. Diven wrote to him:

> You will say nothing to the Erie Railroad people, about the service you rendered me in getting [sic] their bill through the [New York state] legislature. But draw on me at Elmira for five hundred dollars.[7]

Weed worked for the Whig Party and later for the National Republican Party. He was friendly with the rich and powerful of his day, including bank presidents and wealthy railroad barons. His style was consistent with the style of the era—the power of business was synonymous with progress.

This was a time of dazzling wealth and optimism. But many famous misdeeds were perpetrated then. Around 1905, the New York state legislature investigated life insurance companies. It was revealed that the Equitable and the Mutual insurance companies

> maintained a House of Mirth in Albany where legislators relaxed in sensuous surroundings. Andrew C. Fields, chief lobbyist for the two companies, presided over the House of Mirth but was listed in company books as head of Mutual's "supply department." He disappeared when the committee sought to question him about how he managed to spend almost $3,000,000 for printing, stationery, and postage.[8]

LOBBYING BY REFORM GROUPS

It's true that nineteenth-century merchant lobbying was plagued by bribery and scandal. But it must be remembered that at this time there were also many reform movements afoot, such as women's suffrage, prison and educational reforms, and abolition of slavery. Reformers spent much time and effort lobbying for their causes, and some were not above twisting the truth to gain support.

The Temperance Movement, for example, resulted in ratification of the Eighteenth Amendment to the Constitution. This Amendment outlawed the sale of liquor in the United States. It was ratified in 1919, and the resulting "Prohibition Era" lasted until 1933, when the amendment was repealed. The Temperance Movement had begun one hundred years before and included numerous rallies, speeches, pamphlets, the destruction of saloons, and marches on Washington. The chief Congressional lobbyist for the movement at the time was Wayne Bidwell Wheeler, head organizer of the Anti-Saloon League. This group, according to Wheeler, raised and spent in less than thirty years some $35 million to create public interest in the cause. State after state adopted anti-liquor laws.

Wheeler seized upon anti-German feelings of World War I days to impress the public with the need to outlaw alcohol. In his speeches he linked German-Americans prominent in the brewing industry with the hated Germans overseas, thus hoping to twist reluctant drinkers around to his group's point of view. Once, while speaking in Provincetown, Rhode Island, he declared:

> Kaiserism abroad and booze at home must go. . . . Liquor is a menace to patriotism because it puts beer before country. The shot and shell and poison gas of the Germans at the front are more easily met than insidious attacks in camp of the devils of lust, of gambling and of drink.[9]

These absurd claims helped create the climate of opinion that resulted in Prohibition. In this case, distortion was just as powerful a lobbying tactic as payoffs or bribery.

LATE NINETEENTH AND TWENTIETH CENTURY EFFORTS TO REGULATE LOBBYING

Efforts to investigate and regulate lobbying activities in the last hundred years have usually been ill-fated. A resolution requiring lobbyists to register was passed by the House of Representatives in 1875. It remained in effect for one session. A similar bill passed the House in 1913, but died in the Senate. Senator Hugo Black of Alabama, later to become a Supreme Court Justice, introduced another such bill in 1936. It passed both Houses, but was killed in a conference committee of the two houses.

But finally, in 1946, Congress passed the Legislative Reorganization Act. One section, Title III, the Federal Regulation of Lobbying Act, applies to any person who solicits, collects, or receives money to be used principally to influence federal legislation. Under this law, lobbyists must register with the clerk of the House of Representatives and the secretary of the Senate and file spending reports. Penalties are to be imposed on those who don't comply. The idea is that it's okay to petition the government as long as it is not done by slipping some money under the table in return for the "right" vote on a bill.

Unfortunately, there is no one person or agency designated to carry out this law. Furthermore, the wording of the law is ambiguous. Political scientists generally agree that the law is a judicial nightmare, easily evaded by anyone with a little imagination.

We will return to the problem of whether or how to regulate lobbying later on. First let's look at lobbying as it is now practiced.

CHAPTER TWO

The Modern Lobbyist at Work

Lobbies and lobbyists are sometimes called the fourth branch of government—unofficial, unelected, yet very necessary. Nowadays, lobbyists are not, on the whole, unscrupulous or unseemly. Rather, lobbying is a serious professional activity, and its practitioners provide legislators with a variety of important services. In fact, chances are that if there were no lobbyists, we'd have to create them. In France there is even an Economic and Social Council in the government. The Council represents economic and social pressure groups and gives advice on proposed laws.

Similarly, lobbyists here act as consultants on legislation relevant to the groups that hire them. As such, they provide information and support on bills that lawmakers might not otherwise have available to them.

LOBBYISTS AS REPRESENTATIVES

Why has the fourth branch of government become so power-

ful and necessary? The bureaucracy in Washington is complex and enormous. Thomas Jefferson's nation of small farmers passed away a hundred years ago. The U.S. has grown enormous, and hundreds of political units—within counties, cities, townships, and states—now exist, representing thousands of special interests.

In theory, a representative in the House or a state legislature is responsible to his or her own constituency. But voters may disagree when the time comes to allot funds for a war or when an issue such as the busing of students arises. And, of course, the elected official has his or her own personal views to consider as well. So how can a representative find energy and time to listen to *all* the conflicting viewpoints? How can it be decided which faction(s) should prevail?

Lobbying sprang up quite spontaneously in response to this "overload" problem. Lobbyists represent particular constituencies, just as surely as the senator from North Dakota represents that state. They exist because people feel a need to have representation in addition to that provided for in the Constitution, and because legislators simply cannot inform themselves adequately on issues without help from the people who care about a particular problem.

As we have already seen, there are many interest groups in this country. Some are political, such as county governments, some are economic, such as the Teamsters Union, some are humanitarian, such as the Heart Association, and some aim to reform the government, such as Ralph Nader's Public Citizen lobby. But all of them are hungry for a piece of the national, state, or neighborhood pie. Interest groups want to shape government decisions. These decisions may appear in the form of new constitutional amendments, new tariffs, a defense contract, or a research grant, for example. Groups pay a lobbyist to approach the government official most likely to help them collect their piece of the pie. The problem, all too often, is that legislators simply cannot hear all the voices shouting at them for attention. There are so many! Thus people band together, because they believe grouping *works better*. If a lobbyist tells a senator that he represents 15,000 voters—whether it be the membership of a union or all the sugar refiners in the country—the senator is more likely to listen to the lobbyist's point of view. Hence the peace *movement*, the *United* Mine Workers, the *National* Governors Conference, and so on.

LOBBYING AS COMMUNICATION

Former Congressman Emanuel Celler thought of lobbying as a process of communication:

> We may define lobbying as the total of all communicated influences upon legislators with respect to legislation. . . . these messages come to us in a Babel of tongues. . . . But fundamentally, I believe, we all recognize that the touchstone of "good" lobbying and "bad" lobbying is not whether the objectives of persuasion are selfish or altruistic, liberal, or conservative, prolabor or probusiness, but solely and simply whether the message conveyed is intelligible, accurate and informative or cryptic, deceptive and obscure. . . .[1]

Lester Milbrath, in his study, *The Washington Lobbyists*, agrees that in lobbying the major task is to communicate clearly, to create a message, and to choose methods of conveying the message so that elected representatives will receive it favorably—i.e., vote the way the lobbyist wants. Later, we'll discuss the particular methods and tactics lobbyists employ.

THE PROFESSIONAL LOBBYIST'S JOB

Susan Recce is a lobbyist for the National Rifle Association (NRA). She holds a B.S. degree from the University of Delaware.

Prior to becoming a lobbyist, she worked in a congressman's office during his election campaign for the Senate and before that was legislative assistant for another congressman. She is in her late twenties. This is what she says about her job:

> Every day of the week begins at the office unless a hearing or meeting is scheduled early in the morning and a trip to the office is unnecessary. I usually spend from 8:30 A.M. to 11:00 A.M. reading (*Congressional Quarterly, Congressional Record*, crime publications, articles, letters, etc.). Usually after 11:00 I proceed to [Capitol] Hill with a list of people I need to see and carry with me relevant information to hand out. I usually do not make appointments but instead stop by an office and hope that the legislative assistant has a few minutes to spare. Sometimes I will spend the entire afternoon talking with people or return to the office in mid-afternoon, depending on what I need to accomplish for the day. Some discussions with aides may range anywhere from five minutes to an hour depending upon demands on their time and their interest in the issue. On some days, rather than visiting offices, I will attend hearings which may last from two to four hours or make a trip to the Hill to pick up copies of bills and reports. If I have a lot of reading to catch up on or meetings within our division or special projects, I will spend the whole day behind my desk.

Ms. Recce's job involves keeping up to date on the issues—hence all the reading and research—and communicating the NRA position in discussions with staff people associated with Congress. She also sees herself as a representative with a particular constituency:

> As a lobbyist for the NRA, my main responsibility is to repre-

sent NRA's position on issues or specific legislation. Essentially, as a lobbyist I speak on behalf of 1,000,000 NRA members and give the firearms' owners a means of self-expression on a larger scale.

What does she like least about the job?

The stigma that people attach to lobbying and lobbyists as if spokesmen for interest groups have no place in our legislative process and that we are a group of sneaky, underhanded people who use unorthodox means of achieving our goals. Many people have the idea that NRA lobbyists are heavyset old men wearing sidearms and ammunition belts! I will have to say that I have been helping to dispel that myth!

Susan Recce, like all lobbyists, must be familiar with the ways of Congress. The process by which bills become laws is lengthy and complicated, involving speeches, hearings, and bill-drafting sessions. Interest groups participate at all stages of the process, except for the final vote. Activity is likely to be stepped up just before a vote is taken in a subcommittee or committee. The process can be compared to a gigantic debate that includes arguments offered by both sides, compromise, and further argument until a final vote is taken.

SERVICES PROVIDED BY LOBBYISTS

Research

After a bill has been sent to a subcommittee for study, the legislators in the committee may assign members of their staff (aides) to collect data on the issues involved. This is when lobbyists appear with evidence for their positions. Staff members realize that the material they get reflects the prejudices of the lobbyist's group. Nevertheless, such data is especially helpful when the issues are technical, obscure, or complicated. And if the lobbyist has a reputation for accuracy and thoroughness, the staff will appreciate the service rendered. Suppose, for example, that a river pollution bill is being considered by a House subcommittee. A lobbyist for an industry that wants to keep factories pumping into the river in question writes a report about industry efforts to stop the dumping of waste into the water. The Trout Fishing League also hires a lobbyist to research and write a report about the impact of pollution on fish. Whichever lobbyist has a reputation for careful, credible research will have the better chance of winning the support of the committee. Other sources of information that lawmakers use include government agencies, the reference services of the Library of Congress, the executive branch, and sometimes colleges and universities.

Testimony at Hearings

Hearings are usually held on bills a subcommittee is considering. At this time lobbyists plead their cases to legislators much as lawyers argue before a judge and jury. The testimony appears on the hearing record and is available in print to the public at no cost —a good way for an interest group to publicize its cause. Whether testifying at hearings helps the lobbyist's case or not depends on how "overloaded" the committee gets, such as when many different groups want to speak, or the testimony becomes repetitious. And, of course, even if all the members of the subcommittee are present, they may not be listening or they may already be predisposed against a particular lobbyist. There are no guarantees that testimony—even when well researched and effectively presented—will be persuasive.

Collaboration

Sometimes lobbies are so influential that the members of Congress try to gain their support or solicit their opinion. Said one senator:

> I would not hesitate to spur on a pressure group in an activity directed to my colleagues. I might contact some farm groups or some business groups and say to them, "You know, you have been very silent on this tax proposal; I wonder why you haven't spoken up on it.[2]

Lester Milbrath, in his study of lobbyists, says:

> Sometimes members [of Congress] collaborate with sympathetic lobby groups in staging hearings. They review the testimony of witnesses in advance so that the witnesses can prepare answers. They also plan the order of witnesses to maximize the impact on the public of the desired viewpoint. ... officials also store up good will with lobbyists by holding hearings on bills that really have no likelihood of passage, giving the lobbyists an opportunity to appear to defeat the bill. Officials want to "make points" with lobbyists to gain leverage for use in controlling lobbyist behavior. An official who has a store of good will can more freely vote against the desires of a pressure group.[3]

Legislators may also leak information to interest groups or praise them on the floor of the House or Senate to give them favorable publicity.

In addition, members of Congress contact lobbyists for such services as speech writing, preparing reports, drafting bills, answering letters, and entertaining out-of-town visitors.

Building Support for a Bill

Finally, many lobby groups have extensive "grass-roots" connections. That is, they speak for a large portion of the voting public and have communications networks through which they can reach the folks back home. In this way, lobbies such as Common Cause and the National Rifle Association help a legislator build support for his or her favorite bill, for example, by organizing a letter writing campaign.

WHAT TACTICS WORK BEST?

Milbrath asked his sample of lobbyists this question: "What approach do you generally follow to try to get a member of Congress or other public official to agree with your point of view?" About 80 percent said they preferred *direct* methods: testifying at hearings, presenting research results, and personal presentation of viewpoints. Personal interviews were the favorite because it's easier to convey something face to face—the message is less likely to become garbled or forgotten.[4]

Of course, once a lobbyist manages to get an appointment with the right official, he or she has to be *persuasive*. Lobbyists have found that some techniques work well in winning the ear and hopefully, the vote, of busy legislators. After research among lobbyists and members of Congress, Milbrath compiled the following list of do's and don'ts, basic to any good salesmanship: [5]

1. Be personally pleasant and non-offensive. Officials, like all of us, react badly to loud, aggressive, or threatening people.

2. Convince the official to listen to you. The best way to do this is to show that voters want the official to vote your way.

3. Be well prepared and well informed. As one staff assistant put it:

> If he [a lobbyist] wishes to be successful with me or the Senator, he has to be informed. I often know more about the subject than the lobbyist, so I can tell whether he is informed or not. . . . The next most important thing is being able to present the case in a succinct fashion. He's got to be able to handle ideas in an orderly way. If he just runs off at the mouth, you just want to shut him off. The first thing you do is try and figure ways to get out of it. A good lobbyist should be able to cover the subject in twenty minutes or less. . . .[6]

Said another:

> The bird who bends your ear for an hour and wants to buy you a beer is hopeless. A guy should be able to say in fifteen minutes what it is he wants.[7]

4. *Be personally convinced.* A lobbyist who genuinely believes in the case he or she represents is apt to be more convincing than one who couldn't care less. Some lobbyists care only about their salaries, but officials tend to listen more carefully when they think lobbyists believe what they're saying.

5. *Use the soft sell.* A lobbyist who pushes too hard is foolish. The rule of thumb is: If you insist on it being all or nothing, you usually get nothing. Anyone who appears demanding or threatening antagonizes the legislator. Said one Congressman:

> If he says to me: "Here's our story; here's the way our people feel about it. I'd like you to think it over and see if you can go along with us." The fellow who has approached it from that angle has left a good impression and is much more likely to be influential with me than if he approaches it in a demanding way or threatens some damage to me in a campaign. . . . A

member of Congress bitterly resents someone who thinks he can own him or vote him.[8]

6. Leave a short written summary of the case. This insures that the official won't forget the substance of the message.

INDIRECT METHODS

Although most lobbyists prefer direct contact with members of Congress, there are many other ways of influencing the course of a bill. Most of these are *indirect*; that is, they do not involve face-to-face contact with the legislator.

Grass Roots Lobbying

If the hometown voters want a bill passed, you can be sure that the town's representative in Congress will receive mail about it. Many lobbies stir up public opinion through speeches, advertising, and letter writing campaigns to create the appearance of support for their causes. Sometimes this backfires, especially if it's obvious that the letters are inspired by a particular group. Two lobbies that use this tactic extensively—the National Rifle Association and Common Cause—will be discussed later.

Cross-Lobbying

Sometimes several lobbies cooperate in order to get a bill passed or defeated. In the 1960s, for example, the National Rifle Association, the National Wildlife Federation, and the National Shooting Sports Foundation lobbied together against gun control. Cross-lobbying is useful because, when several groups cooperate, there is an appearance of wide support for the cross-lobby position.

Publicizing Voting Records

Again, the lobby that can get voters to pressure legislators has the best chance of being influential. Creating publicity about someone's "good" or "bad" vote sometimes works as a pressure tactic.

Campaign Contributions

Giving money or services to politicians running for office can create problems. Obviously, if a lobby supports a candidate with funds during an election, the candidate may well be inclined to view that lobby's positions favorably. With the cost of campaigning skyrocketing, private contributions are now almost always necessary to pay the cost of getting elected. The Federal Election Campaign Acts of 1971, 1974, and 1976, are supposed to discourage excessive influence by campaign contributors. This issue will be discussed in greater detail in the last chapter.

Entertainment

Milbrath found that when he asked lobbyists and members of Congress how much effect giving lunches and parties had on the course of events, they rated it low. However, because lobbyists are now quite concerned about their reputation (which was badly damaged during the last century), one could expect them to play this down. Former Senator Paul Douglas remarked:

> The enticer does not generally pay money directly to the public representative. He tries instead by a series of favors, to put the public official under such a feeling of personal obligation that the latter gradually loses his sense of mission to the public and comes to feel that his first loyalties are to his private

"YOU'RE TOO LATE. I ALREADY GAVE."

benefactors and patrons. . . . Throughout this whole process, the official will claim—and may, indeed, believe—that there is no causal connection between the favors he has received and the decision which he makes. He will assert that the favors were given or received on the basis of pure friendship.[9]

At any rate, the place of personal obligation in the lobbying process is difficult to assess as a tactic in any systematic way. Probably such favors influence some lawmakers and fail to influence others.

A COMPREHENSIVE STRATEGY

Experienced lobbyists generally combine direct and indirect methods such as these. This involves confronting an issue at all stages of the legislative process and using a variety of tactics. One lobbyist's general strategy, as presented in Milbrath's *The Washington Lobby*, can be paraphrased: he is prepared to compromise, but he realizes he must be careful how and when. He feels the best time is just before the participants' thinking has jelled and positions have become frozen. His strategy is to explore areas of agreement by talking with all members of the congressional committee that will handle the bill. In these discussions he looks for areas of maximum agreement, then drafts a bill to spell out that agreement. He clears his bill in advance with members of the committee, the committee staff, interested parties in the executive branch who would administer it, and representatives from other pressure groups likely to be interested in it. In this way, opposition is headed off in advance, and the bill may well pass easily. The various parties all think they have participated in developing the policy and are therefore unlikely to oppose the bill for personal or other extraneous reasons. This strategy works best when the people involved do not have extremely conflicting interests.[10]

STATE AND LOCAL LOBBYING

The strategy above is that of a lobbyist paid by his group to influence legislation at the national level. Lobbyists may also seek to influence court decisions, voter behavior, and executive branch policy making. Such activity takes place at all levels of government —city, county, state, and federal—and tactics vary according to whether the lobbyist represents an association or a single company.

Oscar Wyatt, for example, is chairman of the board and chief executive officer of Coastal States Gas Corporation in Texas. He wants government and business decisions to favor his enterprise, so he petitions state and local government on behalf of the stockholders of Coastal States Gas, just as Susan Recce, as lobbyist for the NRA, hopes to influence bills in Congress. Wyatt's activities in Texas illustrate that effective lobbying can sometimes be a sharp business tactic. Let's look at some of these activities a little more closely.

In the early 1960s, Coastal States Gas wanted to secure a contract to supply gas for Corpus Christi, Texas. The contract would have made Coastal the city's public utility. As such, the company would be responsible for providing gas to several hundred thousand pilot lights and heat for thousands of homes. The gas contract had to be approved by the city council and then by voters.

Oscar Wyatt used various tactics to win the contract for his company. He wrote to the city's gas advisory committee claiming that Coastal could supply gas to Corpus Christi more cheaply than anyone else. He followed Mayor Ellroy King to civic club meetings and debated the gas question from the floor. Then Wyatt forged a political coalition of minority groups, labor, and white liberals to support his claim that he could supply gas to Corpus Christi more cheaply than his competitors could. As a result of these efforts, Wyatt managed to drum up a record turnout for a special election on the gas contract issue and won his case with the voters. In short, he used grass roots lobbying techniques.

Wyatt has also contributed money to various candidates for state offices and served as cochairman of a dinner honoring a senator from Texas. But one unusual aspect of his involvement in politics was and is his interest in judges. He has given large sums of money to opponents of judges who have ruled against him and is generally credited with the defeat of a San Antonio judge named William Blalock in 1960. Wyatt has also been known to entertain his favorite state district judges at his south Texas ranch.

Why? Oscar Wyatt is a brilliant businessman who knows how to use his knowledge of economics and politics. If lobbying is the effort to influence elected and appointed officials, then Wyatt is a lobbyist *par excellence*. He has realized that the judge's bench can make or break him. Coastal was in and out of courthouses all over south Texas in its early years because gas producers who felt they were being shortchanged by Wyatt were suing. Producers must depend on pipeline builders like Coastal to transport gas to the market. The problem was that occasionally Coastal's figures on how much gas was going in and out of its pipeline were a little mysterious—as when Coastal reported more gas coming out of its pipelines than went into them. Such discrepancies, however, weren't all that uncommon for gas companies because measurement of gas flow is complicated and subject to varying interpretations. Anyway, Wyatt has had good reason to be nice to judges— he might appear in front of them in a courtroom at any time.

Much business, union, and citizen-group lobbying is aimed at federal and state regulatory agencies, those divisions of the executive branch of government responsible for making policies that greatly affect companies. The Texas Railroad Commission, for instance, regulates oil and gas activity in Texas by approving rate increases for public utilities. Accordingly, Wyatt has lobbied this commission when he believed gas rates he'd contracted with cities were no longer profitable.[11] Coastal States is one of thousands of companies who lobby voters, courts, executive departments, and local governments for favors. Lobbying in this country takes place everywhere—morning, noon, and night.

ARE LOBBYISTS COMMITTED?

We have seen that a lobbyist who is convinced of the merits of the case he or she is pleading with legislators has an advantage. But how much interest do most lobbyists take in the causes they represent? When Oscar Wyatt has lobbied on behalf of his company, he has been genuinely committed. But many lobbyists work for more than one company or pressure group. They think of themselves as *lobbyist* first, rather than as a representative of a particular company. A professional lobbyist might advocate many organizations at once. Sixty percent of the lobbyists interviewed by Milbrath reported being mildly committed and about forty percent claimed a strong commitment. Commitment is likely to grow stronger with time, perhaps because once the lobbyist gets more familiar with the issues involved and has helped make policy decisions, he or she becomes identified with that policy. In essence, being a lobbyist is a lot like being a lawyer. But one person contrasted the roles of lawyer and lobbyist in this way:

> It is different in this respect. A lawyer may stretch every point almost to breaking in order to win a case, but when a person is appearing before a congressional committee, he doesn't stretch points; instead he leans over backwards to make sure he is right with his facts. I have to be up there next year and the year after that, and if the members don't trust me, I am sunk. I have seen some people go up there and try to mislead them, but over the long pull the members catch up with them and they get what is coming to them. If you get four or five

senators jumping down your throat on something, you've lost your case and you are finished.[12]

JOB SATISFACTION

As a profession, lobbying can be exciting and useful; it also has moments of drudgery and frustration like any other job. One person said, "Every time I think of leaving this job I reconsider because of the useful services I can perform for my people."[13] Another said: "I love every minute of it. The thing that appeals to me the most is going out and speaking to people of influence. Another thing that appeals to me is the possibility of stimulating a damn good legislative battle. It is stimulating, but it also gives you ulcers."[14] One found the research work frustrating: "It drives me nuts to have to sit down to a time-consuming effort. . . . what I usually do is set it up and turn it over to my secretary. But it is even the setting up that I hate—files and records. . . . I don't do very much of it; I turn as much of it over to her as I can."[15]

Having to curry favor was cited as a disadvantage by this same lobbyist. "The thing that I dislike the most is having to be extremely politic with people who are not really interested and whose motives I have reason to doubt." Another lobbyist says:

> Lobbying to me is all work—no legal skills are needed, and there is no intellectual challenge in it. In lobbying you have got to make sure that you get to the proper ear and explain intricate problems to members of Congress. This is very difficult when you have to be very simple about a very technical matter. You can spend all day on the Hill just seeing two people in it and it is very slow. . . .[16]

Some lobbyists feel that the pressure can sometimes be too great.

> . . . in these urgent situations, there is sometimes a shift in strategy, and you need to contact the members and change what you told them the day before. In these situations months of work is at stake. . . . Perhaps it would not change the vote one bit if I just sat up in my office and did nothing, and yet I feel that I must go down and do everything I can. That is the real drudgery of lobbying.[17]

On the other hand, some lobbyists feel very satisfied.

> I would be quite satisfied to stay in this kind of work for the rest of my professional life. One of the reasons is that in this job, the world is the limit. Our program covers the entire range of things our people would be interested in; thus there are many different ways I can move. I am very content being the biggest frog in a small puddle.[18]

CHAPTER THREE

Lobbying in Action: The National Rifle Association vs. Gun Control

We've now looked at the tactics employed by lobbyists and the services they provide to legislators, as well as shown how lobbyists act as representatives before city, state, and federal lawmaking bodies. Many lobbyists, of course, represent individual firms such as Coastal States Gas and try to bring grass roots pressure to bear on legislators in order to persuade them to vote "their" way. In the early 1960s one such grass roots campaign mushroomed in response to congressional deliberations over weapons control. The question lawmakers were debating was this: Can crime be reduced by controlling weapons? An abundance of evidence indicated that mail-order guns were repeatedly found at the scenes of crimes.

CRIME IN THE EARLY 1960s

The Senate learned, for example, that a mentally ill Los Angeles youth read a magazine advertisement for mail-order guns, ordered and received a revolver, and killed his fourteen-year-old brother with it. In Baltimore a fifteen-year-old boy murdered his family with a mail-order revolver. The list of atrocities grew longer and longer, and though the hearings were concerned mainly with juvenile delinquency, statistics relating to more seasoned lawbreakers also came out. Convicted criminals, it seemed, could and did order guns through the mail, often in violation of state and local gun-control laws. The Chicago police department reported that two mail-order firms shipped 4,069 guns into the city in three years and 25 percent of these guns went to people with criminal records. Twenty-five percent of the people who bought mail-order guns in the District of Columbia also had criminal records.[1] The same was true in other major cities and apparently the guns were mostly foreign imports.

The F.B.I. produced grim statistics. Of the 8,500 homicides reported in 1963, 56 percent were committed with firearms. Of this number 70 percent were committed with revolvers and automatic pistols, 20 percent with shotguns, and 10 percent with rifles. Every year there were 40,000 armed robberies and more than 25,000 aggravated assaults.

An agent hired by the Senate Subcommittee on Juvenile Delinquency infiltrated the Minutemen, a militant underground organization whose goal is to prevent Communists from taking over the U.S. While the agent was in training, he purchased a Russian-made mortar, a Finnish mortar, a bazooka, a rifle with grenade launcher, grenades, and shells—no questions asked.

Further, a Chicago judge said that he filled several bushel baskets every ten days with guns taken from teenagers who appeared in court. "Souvenir" submachine guns that could easily be turned into operating weapons were available through the mail. And so on.[2]

Some states have laws regulating the purchase of weapons, but of course their jurisdiction stops at the state line. As of the early 1960s, the only federal regulations controlling guns were the Federal Firearms Acts of 1934 and 1938, which were both designed to regulate the sort of firearms shipped across state lines during the gangster era of Prohibition. They applied only to arms such as sawed-off shotguns and had little or no effect on weapons' traffic.

Senator Thomas Dodd submitted a bill designed to regulate the mail-order shipment of guns across state lines just four months before Lee Harvey Oswald shot and killed President John Kennedy in Dallas. Oswald bought his mail-order rifle from a Chicago sporting goods store using the name "A. Hidell." He didn't have a permit.

A version of Dodd's bill eventually approved by the subcommittee in March 1966 contained these provisions:

1) Interstate sale and delivery of handguns were prohibited except between licensed gun dealers, manufacturers, and importers.

2) Private individuals could not order a revolver or automatic pistol by mail from a dealer in another state and have it mailed to them.

3) Anyone twenty-one years old or older could buy a handgun over the counter in his or her own state, if he or she provided identification.

4) Long guns (rifles and shotguns) could still be purchased through the mail from out-of-state dealers if they were suitable for sporting purposes. The purchaser did have to provide a notarized affidavit for identification, stating that he or she was over eighteen, and was not a convicted criminal or a fugitive. The dealer was required to send a copy of this affidavit to the purchaser's local police chief.

Two and a half years passed between the assassination of John Kennedy and the 1966 subcommittee vote on the Dodd bill; however, it wasn't until 1968 that any federal gun-control act was approved. Why the delay? It was mainly due to a vast grass roots lobbying campaign organized and conducted by the National Rifle Association (NRA).

THE NATIONAL RIFLE ASSOCIATION AND LOBBYING

The original NRA was founded in 1871 in New York as a nonprofit organization and consisted of a small group of National Guard officers brought together by Colonel William C. Church. Church edited a newspaper called the *Army-Navy Journal*. He believed that the combat performance of volunteer militia units in the U.S. Army during the Civil War was inadequate and envisioned the NRA as a private alternative to the National Guard. He did not want U.S. citizens to depend solely on professional armies for their defense. If the government began persecuting civilians (as Hitler did later in Germany), Americans would still be able to arm and organize to resist. This is of course one of the reasons for the Second Amendment to the Constitution, the amendment that guarantees all citizens the right to keep and bear arms.

In his book, *Gun Control*, Robert Kukla, recently the director of the NRA, explains some other reasons for encouraging civilian readiness. "It has been known for a long long time that no sport and no military related activity affords more in terms of training in self-discipline, steadiness of mind and body, and individual confidence, than marksmanship with rifles and handguns." [3]

Rifle training, Kukla argues, helps build productive citizens because the qualities of good citizenship are learned during rifle training: self-discipline and personal pride.

According to *The NRA Story*, a pamphlet published by the NRA, the organization speaks for law-abiding gun owners in the U.S. They are a special interest group with a special interest in keeping guns available for sporting purposes and for self-defense, and for this reason they have always led the fight against gun con-

trol in this country. They believe gun regulation will not stop crime. The association also offers its members a variety of services: it arranges shooting competitions, certifies instructors in marksmanship and safety, and speaks for conservation of environment and wildlife.

THE AMERICAN RIFLEMAN

What effect did NRA members finally have on the Dodd gun-control bill? By using grass roots techniques employed by many other public interest and special interest lobbies, they were able to delay its passage and limit its content. *The American Rifleman*, chief publication of the group, goes out every month to more than 1,121,000 members. It contains articles on hunting, ammunition, and guns. It also reports continually on the status of legislation concerning guns. (Example: "Why Gun Laws Can't Stop Crime" —June 1975 issue.) This is one way the NRA lobbies for its position.

A regular column, "The Armed Citizen," reprints short news items that illustrate how the mere presence of a firearm can prevent crime, though the editors are careful to say, "Shooting usually can be justified only where crime constitutes an immediate imminent threat to life or limb, or, in some circumstances, property."

For example:

> After locking Graham Cottingham and his wife and grandson in closets, two men tried to open the safe in Cottingham's Dillon, S.C., home. Cottingham, however, was able to free himself and get a pistol he kept under his bed. In the ensuing gunfight, one of the intruders was slain and the other wounded. (Charleston, S.C.—*News and Courier* and *Charleston Evening Post*)

Attorney Frank Farris was awakened about 4:00 A.M. by his wife who thought she heard someone inside their Nashville, Tenn., home. Farris loaded his shotgun and started down the hallway where he confronted a prowler. Farris held the man at gunpoint while his wife phoned police. (*The Nashville Banner*) [4]

A regular feature "What Lawmakers Are Doing" keeps members up to date on firearms laws. Kukla explains that legislative matters were not among the original reasons for the founding of the NRA. Nevertheless, he says, the association was compelled to enter the legislative fray in order to influence where possible, the course of law. The NRA hopes to avoid restraints on good citizens that would have no effect on criminals.[5]

LETTER WRITING

Through the pages of *The American Rifleman*, members are taught to lobby by mail. For example, the June 1975 issue contains an editorial report called "How to Write to Congress." The article refers members to gun-control bills being considered by the House Judiciary Subcommittee on Crime and the Senate Subcommittee on Juvenile Delinquency. "If passed," it claims,

> some of the bills . . . could virtually cripple the shooting sports. You, the individual NRA member, can help prevent this from happening. Past experience has proven again and again that if you tell legislators and public officials the truth about firearms, few objectionable gun bills will ever get off the ground.

The article urges readers to contact Congress right away by letter, telephone, mailgram, or personal visit, and cautions them to include these points in their presentations. They are rules basic to good lobbying:

1. Identify the bill by number and sponsor.

2. Present valid facts and arguments against the bill. . . . know . . . your subject . . . thoroughly.

3. Make your presentation brief, pertinent, clear, and courteous.

4. Be forthright, reasonable, and unemotional.[6]

BULLETINS

The NRA also distributes special bulletins, direct mail, and telegrams to inform the membership about urgent legislative problems. Twenty-six legislative bulletins were mailed to 141,000 members and clubs in eleven states in 1964. The annual report stated that these "NRA members reacted promptly, firmly, and in force. . . . as a result, no severe legislation was enacted." [7]

In 1968, NRA Secretary Frank C. Daniel told the *Congressional Quarterly* that he had no idea how many letters an NRA appeal could generate, but he added that "perhaps half a million would not be too far off." According to *CQ*, the NRA officers were seldom in direct contact with lawmakers, preferring to let the membership try to influence Congress via letters.[8]

CROSS-LOBBYING

As mentioned in chapter two, when a major issue is before Congress, several interest groups will often unite to try to get it passed or defeated. The gun control controversy in the 1960s attracted not only the NRA, but also several wildlife groups—the National Wildlife Federation, the Wildlife Management Institute, the National Shooting Sports Foundation, Inc., and others. In addition, there were many private citizens not affiliated with any group who united to oppose weapons' regulation.

On the other side, the International Association of Chiefs of Police, the American Bar Association, and a number of newspapers (*Washington Post, New York Times, Los Angeles Times*) all supported gun legislation. Towards the end of the debate on the Dodd bill, organization among those favoring strong gun legislation increased dramatically and a strong grass roots pressure campaign was mounted, as we'll see later.

And yet in 1968 *, the NRA was not registered as a lobby group, claiming that its main purposes were educational and that it did not primarily intend to influence legislation. However, the NRA's 1964 annual report boasted:

> Through available reporting machinery, legislation proposed at the federal and state levels usually can be discovered in time to inform our members when effective action is deemed necessary. . . . [on local matters] NRA members . . . must be alert and must act quickly and decisively in a well-organized manner to defeat such threats. Some communities have met the situation by means of a watchdog committee consisting of local NRA members and club representatives who are capable of quickly . . . generating concerted well-timed action.[9]

NRA expenditures for legislative and public affairs rose from $76,563 in 1962 to $157,388 in 1964. Editorial expenses went from $1,315,167 to $1,617,303 in the same period. These figures were reported to members in the annual report, yet expenses were not

---

* The NRA is now registered.

reported to the public under the lobbying law. This is because of loopholes in the law that regulates lobbying. This will be discussed in chapter five.

THE DEBATE

In early 1964, right after John Kennedy's assassination, mail ran eight to one in favor of the Dodd bill. But during hearings on the bill, a flood of letters opposing it appeared.

Members of Congress had difficulty evaluating the situation. Naturally the public felt outraged after the Kennedy assassination. Possibly people's judgment of the bill was blurred in the face of that tragedy. Members of Congress wondered whether a large segment of the public was opposed to the bill or if letters were being generated by a small but loud minority.

NRA president Bartlett Rummel told the Commerce Committee * on January 23, 1964: "We have not drummed up people from all over the country to contact you . . . these communications . . . have more or less arisen spontaneously." However, given the NRA's ability to arouse its members to letter writing, this assertion is questionable.

Senator Dodd appeared before the committee on March 4, 1964, and warned of a concerted effort to kill the bill. He charged the press with contributing to the confusion. When discussion of the bill was postponed (tabled), Dodd accused the committee of "avoidance of the issue," and claimed it was the result of the "almost hysterical efforts" of a "small but loud and well-organized hard-core minority." [10]

Every year following, President Johnson asked Congress for a tough gun-control law, but the bills were always tabled or buried

---

* The debate on gun control dealt with shipment of firearms across state lines; such issues come before the Commerce Committee.

in committee. Johnson wanted a gun law to prohibit the sale of long guns through the mail as well as handguns—except between licensed dealers, manufacturers, and importers. This proposal drew heavy protest from the NRA every time it came up.

In January 1967, a Gallup poll reported that 70 percent of the persons questioned in the survey believed that "laws concerning handguns should be more strict." In 1968 there were two more assassinations. In April, Dr. Martin Luther King, Jr., was shot in Memphis and in June, Senator Robert Kennedy was gunned down in Los Angeles. At this time, debate on the Omnibus Crime Bill was going on. This bill contained a provision for gun control, essentially the same as the Dodd bill. This provision aroused fierce debate.

NRA OBJECTIONS TO THE DODD BILL

What were the NRA's objections to the bill? The argument centered on three issues.

First, it is not the accessibility of guns that leads to crime but the intent of the criminal. In other words, if a person wants to get a gun and use it to shoot someone, he or she will have no trouble doing so; the gun-control law will not prevent this. To support this claim, the NRA cited the unenforceability of existing firearms laws that already prohibited the mailing of concealable firearms. According to available crime statistics, 70 percent of the crimes committed with firearms involved concealable firearms. Thus, the NRA contended, the passage of a new law prohibiting the mailing of handguns would have little effect on this situation.

The second NRA objection was that the bill would infringe on Second Amendment rights. Indeed, Kukla in his book *Gun Control* labels gun control "a euphemism for confiscation."[11] The NRA feared that the bill would lead to a requirement that gun owners be licensed—that they would have to buy a permit from the federal government in order to have a gun. This, in turn, could eventually lead to confiscation of guns by the federal government.

Thirdly, patriotic objections were raised. Harold Glassen, president of the NRA, testified in 1968 that the NRA had trained many men in marksmanship and safety and that many of these men were serving in Vietnam.

> The NRA is rendering a patriotic service to the United States. Today we are engaged in a war to maintain the freedom of the peoples in Southeast Asia. Many young men are today in Vietnam who have been trained with the service rifle at NRA clubs. . . . Gentlemen, this is a great patriotic service. . . .[12]

The NRA also claimed that one of Communism's basic tenets was the abolition of civilian gun ownership; that Lenin, Trotsky, and Stalin, three Russian leaders, believed it was necessary to disarm the public before Communists could triumph. The implication was that people who supported gun control were aiding the Communist party in its plans to take over the U.S. No substantial proof, however, was offered for this assertion.[13]

Harold Glassen issued several additional statements:

> We are witnessing the strange and masochistic spectacle of tens of thousands of normally proud and levelheaded Americans begging the Federal government to take from them by force of law one of their basic civil rights, the right to keep and bear arms.

Glassen further said that:

> [the] NRA voiced the suspicion that control of interstate sales of firearms might be only the first step towards such

measures as registration and we were right. Several bills have been introduced . . . to accomplish national registration of firearms . . . this is the second step.

He concluded:

Now, today, we saw the third step instituted in the form of a bill in the Senate to require a license for the purchase or ownership of firearms. Do we have to say more? Do we have any reason to believe there will not be a fourth and final step in what appears plainly a plan to disarm American citizens? [14]

Thus, the NRA case included unsubstantiated claims about Communism and confiscation. However, the argument that gun control would *not* reduce the crime rate but *would* hinder law-abiding citizens from exercising their right to self-defense attracted much support.

THE CAMPAIGN STEPS UP

The Senate Judiciary Committee approved a gun-control amendment to the Omnibus Crime Bill on April 5, 1968, just after Dr. Martin Luther King, Jr.'s death. It cleared Congress June 6, about twelve hours after Senator Robert Kennedy died, and it was signed by the President June 19. In effect, the bill prohibited the interstate shipment of handguns. But soon after the bill was passed, President Johnson pleaded publicly for an even tougher law banning mail order and out-of-state sales of rifles, shotguns, and ammunition. A number of senators who had previously opposed strict gun control now supported the administration.

Support also came from the U.S. Conference of Mayors and the Republican Governor's Conference. Three major gun and ammunition manufacturers issued a statement on June 15 endorsing the

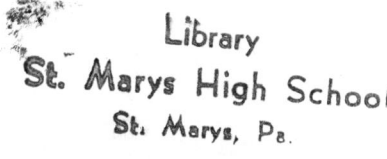

ban on mail-order sales. But the statement also said that states should be allowed to exempt themselves from the mail-order provision and should license owners rather than register individual weapons.

Robert Kennedy's death spurred a massive letter writing campaign all over the country calling for a stronger gun law. Shortly thereafter, letters opposing gun control began to pour into Congress. On June 15, the NRA mailed a two-page letter urging its members to write their senators and representatives to oppose additional gun laws:

> The right of sportsmen in the U.S. to obtain, own, and use firearms for proper lawful purposes is in the greatest jeopardy in the history of our country. . . . indications in the form of statements by some proponents of restrictive gun legislation are clear that their goal is complete abolition of civilian ownership of firearms. The situation demands immediate action by every law-abiding firearms owner in the U.S.[15]

Senator Joseph D. Tydings said in a press release that the letter was "calculated hysteria," and that no proposed bill would keep guns from law-abiding citizens.

Meanwhile, a group called the Emergency Committee for Gun Control, formed by at least thirty national organizations interested in rigid gun controls, opened a Washington office June 18 and vowed to conduct a strong lobbying campaign. The aim of the group was, according to Colonel John Glenn, Jr., the former astronaut, to urge tens of millions of Americans to write letters and petitions, make personal calls, visit Congress—all to encourage passage of a strong gun-control bill. The group used precisely the same grass roots lobbying tactics employed by the NRA. The committee was staffed almost entirely by volunteers who had been working for Senator Robert Kennedy before his death.

Lobbying in Action: The National Rifle Association vs. Gun Control

In October, the Gun Control Act of 1968 cleared Congress. Interstate shipment of long guns was banned to individuals and most people were prohibited from buying guns except in their home state. Dealers were required to record sales; the sale of firearms to convicted felons, indicted persons, unlawful users of drugs, and mental defectives was prohibited.

The debate on the gun-control issue is a good example of how a large interest group can substantially affect the course of law. Using well-tested grass roots lobbying techniques, the NRA succeeded in delaying action on the Dodd bill for several years. And another grass roots lobby developed in opposition—the Emergency Committee on Gun Control—and capitalized on the antiweapon sentiment following the deaths of Robert Kennedy and Martin Luther King, Jr.

Both lobby coalitions represented groups of voters who wanted strong voices in Congress—citizens who wanted representation in addition to that provided by their elected legislators. These citizens relied on lobbyists to speak for them during the gun-control controversy.

The NRA continues to work with Congress on proposed bills. There are some that do call for the purchase of private handguns from owners and threaten confiscation. Some propose federal licensing of individual weapons' owners. Now registered as a lobbying organization with Congress, the NRA maintains its Institute for Legislative Action in Washington. Lobbyists such as Susan Recce, mentioned in chapter two, continue to communicate NRA views to congressional representatives loudly and enthusiastically.

CHAPTER FOUR

In Search of the Public Interest

We've looked briefly at the Coastal States Gas Corporation in Texas and in more detail at the National Rifle Association's efforts to influence Congress. Both are lobbies for special interests. However, lobbying is by no means confined to groups with narrow interests. In the last ten years, the "public" has organized its own lobbies. In so doing people were responding to an undercurrent of feeling about American politics, the feeling that government officials don't represent "the public" interest adequately. The Watergate scandals of the mid-seventies further dramatized this feeling.

RALPH NADER

If anyone could be called the founder of the current citizen's movement, it would have to be Ralph Nader. Nader first became known during his battle with General Motors (GM) in 1966. In his book *Unsafe at Any Speed,* an indictment of flimsy, dangerous

automobiles produced by American manufacturers, Nader had been especially critical of General Motors. He had charged that the new compact, the Corvair, was unstable and a menace on the road, and had carefully documented the many complaints and frustrations felt by numerous Corvair owners in the U.S. The book caused a sensation.

Nader had grown up in Connecticut, the son of a restaurant owner. While still in school, he read the entire *Congressional Record*, thus demonstrating the kind of attention to detail and thoroughness later associated with him. He attended Princeton University, then Harvard Law School, and after a short stretch in a law office, he became interested in traffic safety. A law school classmate, Frederick Hughes Condon, had fallen asleep at the wheel of his car. The car ran off a New Hampshire road, rolled over, and pinned Condon under it, half in the vehicle and half out. He was confined to a wheelchair for the rest of his life. *Unsafe at Any Speed* is dedicated to him.

Nader continued his personal battle for traffic safety by traveling around the country giving speeches and appearing on television to promote safer vehicles. At the same time, a Senate subcommittee headed by Senator Abraham Ribicoff held hearings on traffic safety.

Meanwhile, General Motors began a campaign of harassment against Nader in an apparent effort to intimidate him. In an interview in the *New York Times,* Nader charged that he was being disturbed by annoying telephone calls and that women were being used as lures to lead him into some kind of trap to compromise his reputation. GM spokesmen admitted to an investigation of Nader, but claimed they were only interested in his background, his expertise, and his association with attorneys. Why were they interested in those things? Because, they said, he might be linked to some of the suits that were currently being filed against GM by owners of Corvairs.

When Senator Ribicoff scheduled a hearing to find out the truth,

Ralph Nader became a household word. To most viewers watching the confrontation on TV, Nader was a lone crusader battling a big, powerful corporation. Evidently, GM had resorted to invasion of Nader's privacy because it was frightened by his allegations about the auto industry. The president of GM, James Roche, testified that the investigation had indeed gone far beyond what GM's original statement indicated, and that he had not personally known about or approved the decision to dig into Nader's private life.

Nader testified that he had no connection with the Corvair damage suits, that he only wanted to alert the public to the dangers of the Corvair. He deplored the GM spying and filed suit against the company for invasion of privacy. The suit was settled out of court for $425,000. A wave of public anger at GM helped raise voters' concern for auto safety and a tough Traffic Safety Act was passed in 1966 establishing federal safety standards for cars sold after January 31, 1968.

Perhaps Nader's most important accomplishment, however, was to form the Center for the Study of Responsive Law in 1969. He financed the center with funds from the GM settlement. Here, teams of college students, the famous Nader's Raiders, do basic research. Their purpose is to document cases for needed reforms. Project supervisors direct the research. These task forces have produced studies on mines, pollution, food, old age, and nursing homes. Some of the most damaging evidence the Raiders have collected has been aimed at the federal regulatory agencies, such as the Interstate Commerce Commission (ICC). The ICC is supposed to regulate rail, truck, barge, and moving industries. But federal regulatory agencies are notorious for their willingness to cooperate with the industries they are supposed to be monitoring. The Nader report spared nothing in its analysis of the abuses it found in the ICC. Such studies provide data in support of recommendations aimed at preserving the public interest.[1]

THE PUBLIC INTEREST

The sixties and seventies spawned dozens of groups in addition to Nader's who claim to speak for the "public." Some examples are environmental groups such as the Sierra Club and other reform lobbies such as the American Cancer Society and the National Association for Advancement of Colored People. These lobbies are supposed to counteract what many people feel is excessive influence by groups with narrow constituencies, such as GM or the tobacco industry.

In chapters one and two, we discussed the idea that Americans have geographical representation in government, as with senators, plus private interest group representatives, as with paid professional lobbyists. But nevertheless sometimes a distinction between public and private is difficult to draw. Public lobbies tend to be financed by a variety of supporters; they press for laws that will benefit a large number of people. Consumers, for example, constitute a large constituency.

Still, legislators must sometimes wonder who really speaks for the public. For one thing, it is fashionable for lobbyists to claim that whatever bill they are supporting will benefit the public. This gives them a better chance of convincing a reluctant legislator that he or she should vote for the lobbyist's pet proposal. The National Rifle Association case, for example, includes appeals to patriotism and claims that its proposals benefit all Americans. So also do Nader's Raiders, environmental groups, and so on.

What *is* the public interest, then? Perhaps it is simply the greatest good for the greatest number. No lobby or legislator speaks for *everybody*. Rather, the lawmaker's task is to study the impact of a proposal with everybody in mind. Using the "greatest good for the greatest number" as a criterion, he or she must ask: How many people will it affect? How will it affect them? This sounds reasonable, but there are still problems. What is the "greatest good"? What's "good"?

Problems also arise if a bill violates the rights or interests of a minority group. Some proposed gun-control measures do actually limit the access of weapons to rural residents and law-abiding sportspeople. Is this fair? What's the greatest good in this case?

The point is that someone always loses in the competition for power. Compromise, give and take, find their way into every bill, as indeed they should. But it's difficult sometimes to decide who should give and who should take, and whether the bill does really represent the good of the public.

A second definition of public interest says that the public interest is the sum of all the private interests. That is, there isn't any such thing as a *public*, really. Instead, public interest lobbyists are speaking for the wishes of their membership. Thus, the NRA speaks for its members, Oscar Wyatt for Coastal States stockholders, the Southwest Peanut Shellers Association for its members, and so on.

According to this view, Nader's public interest lobby speaks for those people who want seat belts to be standard equipment on cars. However, it's still true that some lobbies, particularly the ones we think of as consumer oriented or public interest lobbies tend to have a very large constituency, larger, for example, than the number of candy manufacturers. They often speak for people who are not formally affiliated with the organization, and usually address themselves to "large" issues such as traffic safety rather than small issues such as a new tax on candy. Obviously no lobby speaks for everyone. On any issue, the interest of some groups will be advanced and the interests of others will be thwarted. The question remains: Do public interest lobbies speak for the "greatest" number of private interests? How many is that? Or do they speak for a narrow constituency?

Let's look again at the issue of traffic safety. The National Traffic

and Motor Vehicle Safety Act was signed into law September 9, 1966. This was the bill that Ralph Nader lobbied for strenuously as a public interest issue. It provided for the creation of a three-year traffic and motor vehicle safety program in the Department of Commerce. The safety program was to be transferred to the new Department of Transportation in 1967. This department would be responsible for setting federal safety standards.

In 1974, the National Highway Traffic Safety Administration issued a requirement of a mandatory bumper standard. The standard provided for five-mile-per-hour front- and rear-impact protection. (No damage to the car body is to occur at an impact of five m.p.h.) The cost to consumers in 1974 for this bumper standard was $129–$155 per car, depending on the manufacturer. Industry representatives point out that safety standards such as this one had been offered as options on earlier models, but that they did not sell. The reason? Because they increase the price of the car. Now that the federal agency requires the bumper standard on all cars, everyone must pay the extra cost for them, whether or not they would voluntarily select that particular safety feature. The point is that some of the public wants the bumper standard, some of the public does not. A lobby that claims to act in the public interest may succeed in imposing the beliefs of its members on the rest of the public—sometimes at great cost. This bumper standard, by the way, is said to add to the weight of the car and thus increases fuel costs as well as the original sale price.

John Gardner, founder of the large citizens' lobby, Common Cause, which will be discussed following this, has this to say about the public interest:

> Obviously, no sensible person approaches the idea of the public interest without caution. It is a tricky concept. The farmer wants higher prices for his produce and the factory worker wants cheap food. Which is in the public interest? The citizen

as conservationist fights to prevent location of a new power plant in his vicinity, while the citizen as homeowner seeks more and more electric power for his appliances. Which is in the public interest? [2]

He goes on to say that all this makes social policy difficult to formulate. A citizens' group must not assume it has a "divinely inspired grasp" of what the public interest is. Instead, it must debate the other interest groups out in the open, and then use the political process to arrive at a common decision. The key, he says, is to understand and respect the *process* of government and to try to make it more responsive, more effective, more democratic. That's why a citizens' movement, Gardner believes, should be concerned with the structure of government. Could Congress be organized better? How should candidates pay for their campaigns? How should lobbies be required to account for their activities? Gardner thinks these questions are more important than single issues because the way in which they are resolved affects all future issues. It is primarily to ends like these that Common Cause directs itself.

COMMON CAUSE

Common Cause was organized in 1970 as a citizens' lobby. John Gardner, the founder, has a reputation with one critic as being a "first-rate apocalyptic salesman."

After growing up in California, Gardner received a Ph.D. degree from the University of California at Berkeley, served in the Marines in World War II, and later joined the staff of the Carnegie Corporation, where he became deeply involved with education. He eventually served as the Secretary of Health, Education, and Welfare under President Johnson. After a split with Johnson in 1968, Gardner became head of the Urban Coalition, an organization of civic, religious, business, and labor leaders founded in response to the urban riots of the 1960s. He is a man who has moved through many American institutions as a leader as well as someone who is interested in private motivations. He taught psychology at two colleges. Political commentator Elizabeth Drew describes him as "deeply unconventional . . . intense, restless, impatient, and bent on action, and at his most natural can be impulsive and uninhibited." [3]

Gardner has now committed himself to helping Americans gain more influence over what governs them. We can get some idea of his concern for individual initiative by looking at the titles of his books: *Excellence, The Recovery of Confidence, Self Renewal, In Common Cause*. In 1974, he described his number one concern to the *Christian Science Monitor:*

> Whether we have the kind of society in which individuals can participate, feel that they have some importance as individuals and aren't just anonymous numbers, . . . and this has to do with whether we have open, accessible, accountable government, responsive government.[4]

Gardner managed to obtain a quarter of a million dollars in backing money from a few interested individuals to found Common Cause. Newspaper advertisements urging people to join together "in common" to reform the American political system helped attract 232,000 members by October 1971. By February 1974, the membership had swollen to more than 300,000, making Common Cause one of the largest, if not the largest, grass roots, nonpartisan politically oriented movements in American history. Dues are fifteen dollars a year. Membership is largely white and middle class.

The goals of Common Cause are to give the individual citizen a meaningful place in the political process, to abolish wherever possible the usually corrupting influences of money and secrecy in

"THE PUBLIC HAS TOO MANY SPECIAL INTERESTS — FAIRNESS, LEGALITY, DEMOCRATIC REPRESENTATION, A HEALTHY ECONOMY, FREEDOM, SURVIVAL —"

American politics, and to open up the American system of government to public scrutiny.

In the brief time it has been in operation, Common Cause claims credit or partial credit for a remarkable list of reforms, including:

The right of eighteen-year-olds to vote.

Passage in Congress of the Equal Rights Amendment *, an amendment that would prohibit discrimination based on sex.

The requirement that House committee chairpeople stand for reelection by their fellow members. Under the old rules, the person with the most seniority in the majority party automatically became chairperson.

The requirement that House committee meetings be open to the public unless the committee takes a recorded vote to conduct an executive session.

The abolition of residential requirements for voters.

The inclusion of a one-dollar checkoff to be used as a contribution to Presidential campaigns on the Internal Revenue Service forms 1040 and 1040A. This helps Presidential candidates to avoid taking special interest campaign money.

Some critics say that Common Cause takes too much credit for reforms Congress has enacted, that other organizations also contribute to these successes. But part of the Common Cause strategy is to cross-lobby with other groups and to help create the political climate that might allow such reforms—a climate whereby each person can lobby and take initiative in reforming government.

Common Cause is organized for state-by-state action, each state

* The amendment must be ratified by the states before it becomes part of the Constitution.

in turn, by congressional districts. The goal is to have a CC steering committee (see below) in each of the 435 Congressional districts in the country. The membership elects a national board, which in turn shapes members' wishes into specific lobbying goals. The board also deals with organizational issues, financing, and staffing. The state units claim credit for helping pass laws in twenty-five states that curb secrecy in the legislatures or reform campaign financing.

CC TACTICS

Making certain that the public is aware of the CC point of view is part of creating a climate for citizen action through Common Cause. Press conferences are arranged and news releases issued to explain CC activities. CC lobbyists, like most lobbyists, meet with members of Congress to help prepare bills and then to press for votes when the time comes. Volunteers sometimes assist in "head counting"—that is, determining which representatives will come through with the right vote at the right time and which will not. In addition, the newsletter *Report from Washington* reaches all members with information on CC activities and another newsletter, *In Common*, informs activists of current events. Some headlines from the August 1975 issue will help illustrate: "Democrats Duck Open Caucus Vote," "Conflicts of Interest by Representative Sikes," "Financial Disclosure."

The Washington Connection

The local steering committees are loosely organized district groups of CC members who agree to share responsibility for pushing CC positions under the leadership of a coordinator. Specific directions on how to organize locally for best results are listed in the *Action Manual*.

Buy yourself a congressman, a senator —even a president.

It's perfectly legal.

Would you like to have access to high government officials?

Would you like to get special favors not available to the ordinary citizen?

Would you really like to influence the outcome of legislation and rulings that affect your business, your union or your tax return?

Then invest in big campaign contributions. Not only is it legal, it's respectable.

Does this shock you?

It shouldn't, if you look at it from the politician's point of view. In most districts and states it is almost impossible to get elected to Congress today (to say nothing of the Presidency) unless you are either wealthy or willing to obligate yourself to wealthy individuals and/or the special interests through their large campaign contributions.

But maybe it's time to look at it from the citizen-taxpayer's point of view. Maybe it's time to think about the good of the nation. If you believe that, then

The time has come to control campaign finance abuses through publicly-financed elections.

Nothing is going to change in Washington unless we change the way our elections are paid for.

The 1972 elections cost approximately $250 million. If all U.S. taxpayers had paid that bill instead of the special interests, they would have gotten a fantastic bargain. The cost to the American consumer and taxpayer of the resulting corruption is hundreds of times the cost of the election. And who can reckon the cost of undermining the integrity of our government and the loss of faith of the American people?

In 1907, President Theodore Roosevelt recommended public financing of elections. He was ignored. In 1940, the Gallup Poll tested citizen sentiment on public financing. They were against it. But by September, 1973 public opinion had shifted dramatically: 65% were in favor while 21% were opposed.

The people are ready for it, but it isn't that easy. They will have to fight to get it.

Will the Congress act?

In 1973, a clear majority of the U.S. Senate voted for the public financing of both Presidential and Congressional elections.

We are glad to list here the names of the bipartisan group of nine Senators who drew up this historic legislation: Cranston (D-Cal), Hart (D-Mich), Kennedy (D-Mass), Mathias (R-Md), Mondale (D-Minn), Schweiker (R-Pa), Scott (R-Pa), Stafford (R-Vt) and Stevenson (D-Ill).

Unfortunately, their success was later reversed by the Nixon Administration-supported filibuster of their public finance proposal.

In February 1974, the Senate Rules Committee, incorporating much of the 1973 proposal, recommended an excellent public finance bill. Major roles in framing the Rules Committee bill were played by Chairman Cannon (D-Nev), Senator Scott (R-Pa) working closely with Senator Kennedy (D-Mass), and Senator Pell (D-RI).

In the House, the effort for public financing has been led by Congressmen Anderson (R-Ill) and Udall (D-Ariz). More than 140 Representatives have co-sponsored their proposals, but this legislation was successfully bottled up in committee throughout 1973.

The legislation builds upon the Presidential dollar checkoff system developed by Senator Russell Long (D-La) and passed in 1971 under the leadership of Senators Long and John Pastore (D-RI).

Never give a challenger an even break.

In a short time, the House will finally have its first opportunity to vote on public financing of elections. Many will vote no, for a reason they will never tell their constituents. The reason is that the men and women who hold seats in the House of Representatives have a

---

What an investment!

The dairy industry contributed $427,000 to the Committee to Re-elect the President. The dairy industry got back $500,000,000 the first year as a result of a federal increase in dairy support prices.

---

built-in financial advantage over the challengers who will campaign against them. They fear that public financing of elections will bring the challengers onto an equal footing with them.

The most powerful party in Congress is neither the Republican Party nor the Democratic Party. It is the party of those who now hold office: the Incumbency Party which operates a near monopoly under the guise of free elections.

In the 1972 general elections, more than 95% of the House incumbents who ran won re-election. The same was true in 1970 and in 1968. The system, as it is now set up, practically guarantees the re-election of the incumbent.

Here is why: A Common Cause study of the 1972 Congressional campaigns showed that incumbents, regardless of party, averaged a 2 to 1 financial advantage over their challengers, through campaign contributions.

The study revealed that organized special interest groups gave incumbents approximately three times as much as they gave their opponents. Money flows to those who have the power.

Add to this what the incumbent Congressman enjoys in the free mailing privilege (worth about $50,000 a year in postage), travel allowances, TV/radio broadcasts, and other publicity-generating devices, and you will understand why the incumbent is at a tremendous advantage.

This represents the biggest obstacle we have to enacting a new system of public financing for federal elections. By supporting this reform, Members of Congress will be voting to give up their present financial domination of campaigns. They must overcome their own self-interest in order to vote for the nation's best interests.

Our system of representative government is based on having a real choice among elected leaders. When competition disappears, the accountability of the elected official to his constituents disappears with it. The citizen's voice is not heard.

What you can do:

Write your Congressman and ask him where he stands on these four key points:

1. Public funds for Congressional and Presidential elections.
2. An independent enforcement agency.
3. Strict ceilings on contributions.
4. Reasonable limits on campaign spending.

If you want to do more, become an active member of Common Cause.

Common Cause gets results.

We played a major role in successfully lobbying for the 1971 campaign financing law. We forced disclosure of the secret contributors to the Committee to Re-elect the President.

"When the history of Watergate is written, Common Cause will take its place with the Washington Post, Federal Judge John Sirica and others who are fighting corruption in high places."
Richard Rodda, Political Editor
The Sacramento Bee, Sacramento, Cal

Right now we are in the thick of the battle to enact legislation for the public financing of elections.

Common Cause gets results, and here is why:

Our program is being proved correct. The time has come for a citizen's lobby that works to make the government accountable to the people.

We now have a membership of 300,000. Since many of these are husband-and-wife memberships, the actual number of members is closer to 400,000.

Our members are dedicated. When Congress made no provision to adequately monitor the 1972 campaign spending law, over 1,000 Common Cause members quickly volunteered to do this difficult and time-consuming job.

Our membership is not confined to a few parts of the country. We have members in places like Fayetteville, Ark., Cheyenne, Wyo., Meridian, Miss., Oskaloosa, Ia. and Carson City, Nev.

We combine citizen pressure at home with a highly professional staff of lobbyists in Washington. And we concentrate our energies.

We pay our own way. We don't depend on big contributors; the money to support our work comes from our own members who pay dues of $15 a year.

Everybody's been organized but the people. Now it's our turn.

—**John W. Gardner**

If you will send in your check with your membership application, thereby saving us bookkeeping costs, we will send you a free copy of John Gardner's latest book, "In Common Cause." Paperback. 130 pages.

☐ Check enclosed ☐ Bill me

Common Cause
2030 M Street, N.W., Washington, D.C. 20036
Tel: 202-833-1200

I would like to become the next member of Common Cause. I understand that my annual dues will be $15 which will help support the work of the organization. (Husband & wife may both join under a single membership.)

☐ I want to do more. My check also includes a contribution to Common Cause of $____

☐ Miss ☐ Mr ☐ Ms
☐ Mrs ☐ Mr & Mrs.

Address
City_____ State_____ Zip_____
Phone number (Give area code)

Common Cause

Suppose that the House of Representatives is considering a bill on water pollution. The bill would involve cleaning up a large lake near your city. The new law would be expensive but your Common Cause unit has decided that it would be worth it. How do you, as a private individual, fit into the CC effort to get this bill through Congress?

CC has set up a rapid, direct, two-way communications system between staff and volunteers in Washington and active members in the local districts. It is called the Washington Connection. If you were a local coordinator, your phone would ring one morning and the Washington Connection would inform you that this particular water pollution bill is pending in the House; perhaps it is bogged down in committee. It so happens that your representative is on the committee.

Your first task is to alert the steering committee, which then, through its telephone coordinator, alerts the entire CC membership in the district, especially when immediate action is needed. You tell the members to write letters to their representative and senators. The *Action Manual* emphasizes that the issue must be described accurately in these letters. The local committee keeps a file of information—facts and figures—to support the CC position.

You, as local coordinator, would contact the editor of your local newspaper, reporters from TV and radio stations, and places where speakers might be arranged to explain the CC position (universities, civic club meetings, environmental group meetings, and so forth). The manual suggests that if you go to a public meeting, it's a good idea to ask a question to draw attention to the CC position. However, it cautions against threats. "Be temperate, even if you do not care for your representative. You will accomplish more by remaining calm and sticking to the point. . . . No one likes to be bullied, including politicians."[5]

Letters

The success of a large grass roots lobbying effort often depends on whether a movement's members or followers write effective letters and on the timing of the mail campaign. (Is the bill nearing a vote in Congress?)

You'll recall the letter writing instructions offered by the NRA in the *American Rifleman,* mentioned in chapter three. The NRA's ability to generate a half-million letters on short notice is its most powerful lobbying tool.

Similarly, CC's *Action Manual* contains specific directions on how to write letters. They are useful, because as a private citizen you can follow the suggestions, whether or not you belong to a particular lobbying group. They could have been written by the NRA or any grass roots lobby.

1. Keep the letter short. . . . Type if you can; otherwise write clearly.
2. Write it in your own words, and include your own thoughts.
3. Cover only one issue; save other issues for later letters.
4. Show your familiarity with the subject and with the current status of the legislation (mention the bill number if possible). This will indicate that you are serious about the issue, unlike the casual, uninformed correspondents who produce the bulk of constituent mail.
5. Be specific as to what you want your representative to do.
6. Give reasons for your position. Cite your own experience and observation if possible. If the bill has a local impact, indicate that fact so that your representative realizes that the bill has a direct effect on his or her district.
7. Ask your representative a direct question about his or her own position on the bill. You want to receive a clear answer, not a form letter.

8. Don't mention your membership in Common Cause or any other organization (unless it's directly related to an experience you're describing). The individual citizen's letter is what counts, not the letter that has obviously been inspired by an organization.

9. If you can, mention your legislator's vote on a recent issue to show your awareness of his or her record.

10. In general, be helpful rather than threatening. You can best show your genuine concern for the issue by offering to provide further information on the subject.

11. When the legislature is in session, address all letters to your representative in Washington or your state capital. At other times write them in care of their home address, if available.

12. Finally remember: ANY LETTER IS BETTER THAN NO LETTER! Postcards are second-best; it's hard to get enough information on them.[6]

Telephone Calls

The *Action Manual* asserts that phoning your representative is a legitimate method of lobbying as long as you remember to be concise, state your points and the evidence you've gathered, and say what action you'd like to see taken. Speak to an aide if the representative is out.

Coalition Building

In addition to urging individuals to put pressure on legislators, like-minded groups can be contacted for help, for cross-lobbying. In the case of a water pollution bill, places to look for support might be environmental groups, tourist groups, the fishing industry, and so on. The more support that can be mustered, the better luck the bill will have.

Following Up

As coordinator of your district effort, you would be in touch with the Washington Connection often. As events break, you would be asked to organize follow-up phone calls, asking Common Cause members, "Did you write that letter you promised?" "Did you go to the meeting we told you about?"

Using this system, a message can reach hundreds of Common Cause members in a very short time.

PROPOSITION NINE

Using techniques such as these, Common Cause lobbied for the passage of a measure known as Proposition Nine which appeared on the California ballot during the 1974 elections. The proposition was designed to increase public disclosure of lobbying activities and to monitor campaign spending. Common Cause helped draft the proposal, gathered petitions on its behalf, and publicized the issues throughout the state. Proposition Nine won more votes than any candidate despite opposition from business groups and the state American Federation of Labor–Congress of Industrial Organizations (AFL–CIO). It included these provisions:

> Full public disclosure of lobbyist spending; prohibition of lobbyists giving campaign contributions to public officials *;
>
> Limits on election spending by candidates for statewide office;
>
> Full public disclosure by officials at all levels of California

---

* It's interesting that in 1971, CC reported spending $847,850 on lobbying, more than any other organization. This may be because it is more scrupulous than most about complying with federal registration requirements, or that it just spends more than other lobbies.

"...THEN THE UGLY, DREADFUL CAMPAIGN REFORM BILL GRABBED THE POOR, DEFENSELESS LOBBYIST AND TOOK AWAY HIS INFLUENCE..."

government of financial holdings that might bias their official actions;

Full reporting of contributions to and spending by candidates for office; prohibition of cash or anonymous contributions of fifty dollars or more; and

An independent Fair Political Practices Commission to enforce the new law; citizens permitted to sue if the state does not enforce it.

The California branch of the American Civil Liberties Union (ACLU) did not take a stand on the issues involved because its members were hopelessly divided. Those who opposed the bill feared that disclosure provisions might lead to harassment by employers of workers who disagreed with them. They also thought that the limit on spending meant that people who were not well known would be at a serious disadvantage, for example, a movie star running against a plumber. Harold Williams, statewide coordinator of Common Cause at the time, said:

> I understand the problem on the other side. But if we don't have widespread disclosure and an independent commission, we leave open the possibility for widespread corruption like Watergate, the milk scandal, and the ITT case. In the final analysis, one has to opt for emphasis on public good rather than private protection.[7]

Proposition Nine is especially important because of its implications for lobbyists and for candidates at all levels of government—state, local, and federal. In the next chapter we'll discuss the reasons many people felt this type of legislation was needed.

You'll recall earlier discussion in this chapter about the public interest. According to one definition, "public" is "the greatest good for the greatest number," though defining "greatest good" can be difficult. An alternative definition calls the public interest the sum of private interests. This definition claims it is impossible for any one lobby to speak for the public; a citizens' lobby in this case, speaks for the wishes of its members or stockholders—thus taking its place alongside the NRA, Coastal States Gas, and other special interest lobbies.

In the debate over Proposition Nine, some members of the ACLU felt that the threat to privacy was not in the public interest. Common Cause believed that Proposition Nine would serve the public interest.

Clearly, Common Cause and Ralph Nader's Public Citizen lobby don't speak for everybody. They lobby on issues their members believe to be important. Since the public good is defined differently by different lobbyists, it's a good idea to join the lobby that defines it the way you define it and to recognize the limits of the concept.

Common Cause, using grass roots lobbying techniques similar to the National Rifle Association, sets in motion citizen response to specific legislation, thus influencing the course of bills. The big difference between the two lobbies, of course, is that the NRA is a special interest group, concentrating its attention on a narrower set of issues—those involving gun control. Common Cause is a "public" interest group, and concentrates on a much larger set of issues—issues relating to the structure and process of government, as well as bills its membership believes to be in the public interest.

CHAPTER FIVE

Regulating Lobbying

The Watergate scandals and the resignation of President Nixon made the mid-1970s an especially favorable time for reform. Proposition Nine in California, discussed in the last chapter, was one of many legislative packages designed to enable the public to monitor the activities of government and special interests. In this chapter we will deal more closely with what can and should be done to regulate lobbying practices.

HOW EFFECTIVE ARE LOBBYISTS?

Is lobbying good or bad? How should we deal with whatever may be bad about lobbying without sacrificing contributions lobbyists make to our political system? Do special interest groups really have the power that the media and public assign to them? Before analyzing efforts to "open up the system," let's take a closer look at the effects of lobbying.

First, lobbying must be placed in context—lobbyists work to influence lawmakers, but lawmakers are influenced by a number of other things: the President, Congress, the executive agencies, political parties, opinion leaders, the media, voters, personal conviction, friendship, money, ethics, self-esteem, and so on.

Lester Milbrath, in his study of Washington lobbyists and Congress mentioned earlier, reports that half of his respondents credited the executive branch, led by the President, as having the most influence on policy. Other factors mentioned most often were voters and Congress. In wrestling with this question, one lobbyist said:

> I don't know where in the world I would fit the lobbyists as a group. Some of them have been up here for years battling lost causes. On the whole and speaking of all lobbyists in general, I think they are a lot less effective than most people believe.[1]

It's certainly true that the President's influence has become especially important since the Franklin Roosevelt administrations. The President, because of his prestige, his ability to command attention in the media, and the enormous resources at his disposal is capable of leading public opinion toward support of his legislation a long time before it comes up in Congress. In addition, the President has numerous personnel and legislative liaison people in each executive department. It is quite customary for a congressional committee to seek information from the executive department concerned with the bills it is considering. And the executive branch keeps tabs on Congress. Lobbying by executive officials is pervasive and steady, especially since World War II. Yet they do not have to register under federal regulation of lobbying laws.

Under President Johnson, for example, each department and agency provided the President's office with a written report each week of that department's activity with Congress over the previous week and what its plans were for the week to follow. Executive officials walk the halls of Congress in search of commitments and votes, like other lobbyists.

Federal law prohibits lobbying with federal funds. And yet when legislative liaisons meet with Congress, flood committees with proposals and information, and encourage public opinion in the direction of a particular bill, they are obviously lobbying. Representative Thomas Curtis complained:

> So let's have a cessation of this business of the executive officials, Cabinet officers, coming into Congressmen's offices. They don't even come before the committees, they come to visit you in your office to sell you on this particular point of view. And I say if you want to say this, say it out in the public where the (other) side can hear you, don't come in and talk to me privately unless there's a basic reason.[2]

Although the President has great influence, members of Congress and lobbyists both claim that the views of voters are uppermost when it's time to cast votes in Congress. It's for this reason that many lobbying groups rely on grass roots campaigns that generate thousands of letters at crucial moments in the lawmaking process.

Representatives of large organizations such as labor and farm groups report that they are asked for their opinion more often than are other lobbyists. This reflects, again, congressional concern about voters. Farm and labor lobbyists represent large numbers of voters and the Southwest Peanut Shellers simply do not. So voters and the President probably influence legislation more than lobbyists do.

Milbrath suggests that the reason lobbyists are not as important as most people think is that they don't have much to offer a representative in return for his or her vote, and they don't punish lawmakers significantly if they vote "wrong." The usual enticements the public associates with lobbying—parties, lunches, entertainment—are not considered by most representatives to be enticing at all. This kind of favor (at its worst, outright bribery) is considered too dangerous or too boring by lobbyists and officials to be used very much. Of course it's difficult to measure the extent to which small favors succeed in affecting a vote in Congress. But it seems reasonable that free lunches wouldn't have much effect.

Lobbyists do have a kind of nuisance impact, says Milbrath.

> They can make life somewhat unpleasant for officials who do not go along with them: It is embarrassing to vote against someone who is watching; it is difficult to vote against a group that has sent six thousand letters; it is hard not to listen to someone who is very persistent; it is hard to stand up to scorn by the public media. On small matters these nuisance factors may have considerable impact; they may even be decisive; but on matters of large public import, such factors are rarely, if ever, of any great importance.[3]

If lobbyists have little effect on big issues, they can and do affect the details of such bills as traffic safety or tax reform; they affect how fast some bills go through Congress, the content of specific sections of bills, and so on.

If an issue affects only a small group or an obscure segment of society, lobbyists often have their way. A member of the Ways and Means Committee of the House told a story about two lobbyists who appeared before the committee to argue about when the tax on whiskey should be due and payable. Each was the representative of a whiskey distillery and each was simply seeking a competitive advantage over the other; there was nothing in it for or against the public. The press ignored the issue. After listening to the arguments made by both sides, the committee voted. Milbrath concludes, "Lobbying may have been important on this bill, but was the bill really important?" [4]

So far, we've said that lobbyists have little effect because they are only one of many influences on legislators and because they aren't usually powerful enough to offer a legislator the kind of reward he or she might respond to. Another possible factor that diminishes the effectiveness of lobbyists is the *number* of pressure groups. Because there are so many, there is little danger that one of them will have more influence than the others. Thus, when the NRA speaks against a gun-control measure, a group such as the Emergency Committee for Gun Control will usually spring up to argue the other side. The problem here is that too often some group is left out of the debate. People may be weakly organized, lack money, or simply not present their case very well. Then they have to rely on Congress to produce arguments that will counter special pressure. That, of course, is uncertain. It's easy for Congress to ignore quiet segments of the electorate, especially if another group is very outspoken.

Milbrath concludes that special interest pressure isn't necessarily a bad thing, especially since lobbying usually doesn't work without the approval of voters. The one thing that always influences a member of Congress is the wishes of constituents. If a lobbyist can show that a vote this way or that will affect the legislator's chance of getting reelected, that's the kind of reward-punishment he or she will understand. That's why grass roots lobbying is so important. However, Milbrath's study is based on what lobbyists and members of Congress say about themselves. All the lobbyists he interviewed were registered; thus, his group may be more law-abiding and ethical than most. Obviously the people in his sample group wanted to sound like responsible lawmakers and law-influencers. They would surely prefer not to admit that pressures of a questionable nature (favors, entertainment, personal obligations) were high on their list or that voters weren't always uppermost in their minds.

So much money is spent on lobbying that somebody must think it's worth it. One congressional committee concluded that the business of influencing government was a billion-dollar-a-year industry!

HOW CLEAN IS LOBBYING?

Certain broad rules apply to politics in America. When they are violated, politics is viewed as dirty. First, public decisions should be made in full public view. Efforts to operate in secret are considered to be corrupting, as are efforts to influence a decision for private gain. Second, each person should have one vote that is counted equally; someone who possesses large amounts of money or property should, in the end, have no more power over lawmakers than anyone else. Third, lawmakers must calculate the merits of a particular case rather than their own personal gain when voting.[5]

From all accounts, lobbying is simply not the insidious vote-buying spree the media often portray it to be. Sensational bribery stories and blackmail scandals are genuinely exceptional. Of more concern are subtler, harder to measure influences, such as friendship, indirect gifts, and services such as the use of private planes.

CAMPAIGN CONTRIBUTIONS

One famous instance in which the rules of clean politicking were violated is the dairy scandal of 1971. This incident illustrates what is today a much more important influence on policy than small favors and job offers—the ability of a lobby to aid an officeholder through campaign contributions. In this way, the most important influence—voters—can be swayed for or against a candidate. The candidate's job is at stake.

In 1971 the dairy industry demanded that the government raise the guaranteed price it paid farmers for certain milk products. The government supports milk prices by guaranteeing the dairy industry it will buy up a certain amount of dairy products annually. These items are regularly used for surplus food programs such as school lunches. Under this system, the government withdraws a percentage of the total quantity of dairy products from the marketplace. Whenever a portion of marketable goods is removed, a shortage is created, and the price on the remaining products increases for consumers. Thus, when the dairy industry asked the government to increase the support price in 1971, the result would be an increase in the price of retail foods available to consumers in the marketplace. Department of Agriculture officials were also predicting it would lead to the accumulation of surpluses of milk, because the higher price would cause sales to go down. On March 12, 1972, Clifford Hardin, who was then Secretary of Agriculture, announced that the price would not go up.

Two weeks later, on March 25, the administration yielded to dairy lobby demands. Secretary Hardin claimed he'd found new evidence and announced a 6 percent price boost, exactly what the dairy industry had asked for. Why?

The dairy lobby raised one million dollars for political campaigns in its first two years of fund-raising. Five hundred thousand dollars of it was spent in the elections of 1970. When the question of the price increase first came up, lobbyists for the dairy industry turned to those officeholders whose campaigns they had subsidized. After Hardin's first announcement, the industry drafted a bill that would have made the increase compulsory. Thus, the Agriculture Department would no longer have control over whether or not the price rose. In the House, 116 members, of whom 50 had received contributions from the dairy industry for their campaigns, jumped on the bandwagon as cosponsors. In the

"Your honor, they are all highly moral people and they only followed the biblical adage — 'It's better to give than take'"

Senate, the bill had 29 sponsors. Twelve of them had run for election in 1970; eight had received dairy industry contributions.

On March 22, two weeks after the initial rejection of the dairy price increase, the dairy lobby made a big contribution to President Richard Nixon's reelection campaign committee—a total of $255,000, paid in installments. The day after their first big contribution, dairy and farm representatives were invited to the White House. In a letter to one of his group's members, William Powell, president of the Mid-America Dairymen, described the meeting as follows:

> We dairymen as a body can be a dominant group. On March 23, 1971, along with nine other dairy farmers, I sat in the Cabinet room of the White House, across the table from the President of the United States, and heard him compliment the dairymen on their marvelous work in consolidating and unifying our industry and our involvement in politics. He said, "You people are my friends, and I appreciate it."
>
> Two days later an order came from the U.S. Department of Agriculture increasing the support price of milk . . . which added from $500 million to $700 million to dairy farmers' milk checks. We dairymen cannot afford to overlook this kind of economic benefit. Whether we like it or not, this is the way the system works.[6]

When these contributions were revealed to the public, the dairymen received a lot of unfavorable publicity, as did the Nixon administration. This kind of payoff, though not always so large or so flagrant, happens often enough, and is much more common than the outright buying of votes on specific bills. Citizens have the right to help elect the candidate of their choice, but that right is not usually exercised unless the contributor approves of a candidate's past or promised actions. Congressman Kong may not know himself whether a contribution is due to his superior statesmanship or whether it reflects approval of his votes in Congress. If the transaction is made in full public view, is it really improper? Voters are free to decide whether they want to reelect someone who is a tool of the dairy interests or not. In this case, public outrage accompanied the publicizing of the dairy lobby's crude effort to buy Nixon's support, and probably gave impetus to the movement to regulate campaign contributions.

COSTS OF CAMPAIGNING

It is unfair to discuss the pressure on candidates from campaign contributors without mentioning the costs of campaigning today. The turning point for campaign expenses was the Civil War, after which corporate money began to buy political favors on a grand scale. Politicians often went along eagerly. In 1903, for example, a Standard Oil agent (a member of Congress), checking on a "loan request" from a senator, wrote to the company's vice-president, John Archbold: "Do you want to make the investment?"—meaning "The senator wants to borrow money for his campaign. If we lend it to him, and he wins the election, he'll support our industry on crucial votes in Congress. The loan is an investment in the senator's support for our interests."

Where do campaign contributions go? To salaries for campaign workers, stamps, envelopes, billboards, barbecues, whistle-stops in small towns. Air travel costs a fortune. One senate staffer said he averages twenty-two trips home per year at a cost of $10,500! And nowadays, candidates use television, radio, and newspapers as their primary source of publicity—all enormously expensive activities.

In 1952, when Dwight Eisenhower ran for President, the total spent in national election campaigns was $140 million, according to the Citizen Research Foundation. In 1968, all national cam-

'IT'S FOR THE PROTECTION OF THE CANDIDATE. GENTLEMEN, LET'S START NOW- KEEP YOUR CONTRIBUTIONS READY'

paigns cost $300 million; the increase was largely due to the cost of TV spot commercials. Not surprisingly, then, in the 1970 senatorial elections, of the fifteen major candidates in the seven largest states, eleven were millionaires. The four who were not, lost.[7]

H. Ross Perot, head of Electronic Data Systems, Inc., of Dallas, Texas, supplies the government with data processing for Medicare and Medicaid programs. These programs are overseen by the House Ways and Means and the Senate Finance committees. In 1974, Perot contributed $58,900 to twenty members of Congress who were associated with these committees. He also gave $2,500 to the chairman of the House Appropriations Subcommittee that handles administrative funds for the Medicare and Medicaid programs. Eleven of Perot's contributions were made after the November elections were over; two of them went to Congressmen who had just been named to the Ways and Means Committee for the first time. Some campaign finance bills Congress has considered propose a $1,000 contribution limit. Had there been such a limit on Perot's gifts, two-thirds of his total contributions would have been eliminated.[8]

Once again, we must ask: Do people perform in Congress a certain way because they receive a contribution? Or do they receive a contribution because they have already voted the right way? The gist of the matter is this: If you elect the right person to Congress, you might not even have to lobby.

Whenever such obvious vote buying becomes public knowledge, we are forced to wonder how many hundreds of other such instances occur behind the closed doors of congressional meeting rooms. Probably most lobbyists do follow the rules—they stay open, they don't buy votes with bribes or gifts, they provide lawmakers with information and research. Still it's clear that any effort to purify lobbying will have to deal with campaign contributions. Such money has real power at the polls—and hence with lawmakers.

THE CAMPAIGN FINANCE LAW

With campaign costs continuing to rise, it is at best idealistic to expect candidates to turn down large sums of money from private contributors. However, several laws have been passed recently that seek to discourage reliance of Presidential candidates on large or powerful interests such as the dairy lobby or H. Ross Perot. Unethical financing, it is hoped, will be avoided by funding election campaigns with *public* money.

In December 1971, an amendment to a tax bill was passed that allows taxpayers to contribute one dollar of their yearly federal income tax to a Presidential election campaign fund. Money from the fund is available to qualified candidates. Also passed in 1971 was the Federal Election Campaign Act, which requires stricter disclosure to the public of the sources and amounts of campaign funds. This act applies to races for President and Congress and was a significant factor in exposing payoffs during the Watergate controversy.

In 1974, the Federal Election Campaign Act was extended to cover Presidential primaries. Once a candidate for nomination raises $5,000 in each of twenty states in private contributions of no more than $250 apiece, he or she will qualify for public funds to match.

Candidates for nomination are eligible for up to five million dollars from income tax check-off funds and can spend up to twelve million dollars. Presidential nominees can spend up to twenty million dollars total, but they cannot mix private and public financing. If a nominee chooses full public funding, he or she cannot accept private contributions.

The law also limits contributions from individuals, organizations, political committees, and national and state party organizations in Presidential and congressional races. Provisions were made for enforcement.

In January 1976, the Supreme Court ruled that substantial portions of the 1974 act were unconstitutional. The Federal Election Commission, the act's enforcing agency, created constitutional problems. The Court also ruled that campaign spending limits were in violation of the First Amendment guarantee of free expression. The Court stated:

> A restriction on the amount of money a person or group can spend on political communication during a campaign reduces the quantity of expression . . . because virtually every means of communicating ideas in today's mass society requires the expenditure of money.[9]

The Court, however, upheld the public financing system for funding Presidential campaigns, upheld the requirement that recipients make public these contributions, and permitted limitations on contributions.

PROBLEMS WITH THE 1974 LAW

The American Civil Liberties Union and others had maintained that requiring disclosure of small contributions threatened one of our most fundamental freedoms—the right to a secret ballot. Suppose a voter wants to support a candidate who opposes the policy or interests of the person he or she works for. That voter might not want the contribution made public. Business people who depend on their customers' goodwill might not want to disclose their support of an unpopular candidate.

Other opponents of the law claimed it favored those already in office because they find it easier to raise money and thus to qualify for public funds. A third objection is a more general one—that the enforcing agency would be overly influenced by established political parties, the Democrats and Republicans, and might not protect the interests of independent and smaller parties.

THE CAMPAIGN FINANCE LAW OF 1976

After the Supreme Court decision, Congress set to work drafting the Federal Election Campaign Act Amendments of 1976. President Ford signed them into law in May 1976. This new law clarifies the role and powers of the Federal Election Commission, and slightly alters disclosure requirements and dollar limits on campaign contributions. It also requires that most funds solicited by corporate and union groups be raised by mail, anonymously. Thus, employees do not have to divulge their political contributions to their employer or union. The law also limits campaign spending by Presidential candidates to no more than $50,000 of their own or their family's money if they accept public financing.

The intent of the campaign finance laws is to reduce the influence of special interest group money, money spent secretly on government officials. The laws limit the dollar amount of contributions, require that the sources of campaign funds be made public, and provide a public source of campaign monies.

Let's look now at a second way that excessive lobby pressure might be reduced: changing the structure of government itself.

THE STRUCTURE OF CONGRESS

Any effort to control the lobby process must deal with some of the institutions that encourage "excessive" or "secret" influence by special interests. One of these institutions is Congress, especially because of the way it is organized. The seniority system, for example, has traditionally awarded the chair of committees to the highest-ranking member (in terms of length of service) of the majority party, and thus helps block new, nonestablished members and their favorite interest groups from obtaining power. This system is slowly being altered. The rules of the House of Representatives were recently changed to provide for the election of committee heads.

Another problem with the structure of Congress is that certain segments of the public, especially minorities and women, continue to be underrepresented, thus creating a need for their voices to be heard through lobbyists. If Congress were more truly representative, there might be less reason for lobbyists to exist.

THE LOBBYING ACT OF 1946

So far, the principal effort to regulate lobbying directly is the 1946 law. The provisions are based on the assumption that it's okay to petition the government as long as it is done openly and records of the activity are available to the public.

As mentioned in chapter one, this law is part of the Legislative Reorganization Act of 1946. It requires that any person

> who shall engage himself for pay or for any consideration for the purpose of attempting to influence the passage or defeat of any legislation by the Congress of the United States shall . . . register with the Clerk of the House of Representatives and the Secretary of the Senate.

Anybody who seeks to influence legislation is required to register as a lobbyist, but only if he or she is being paid. The "anybody" includes individuals, partnerships, associations, corporations, and the like, so that all pressure groups fit the definitions. On registration, the lobbyist must provide factual information about the scope of his or her activity: name, business address, name of employer whose interest is being pursued, how long he or she has been employed as lobbyist, salary, who pays the salary, money being given for expenses, what expenses are being in-

'No, leave the door open'

cluded, what legislation the lobbyist is interested in, who is receiving the money and for what purpose. All this sounds reasonable and, if the law worked, would provide the public with information about money and contacts that it needs when evaluating the impact of lobbyists on Congress. But the law contains a gigantic loophole: the statute applies *only* to people and organizations whose *principal purpose* is lobbying.

Courts and lobbyists have had fun with this. How does one define "principal purpose"? Not surprisingly, many representatives of associations claim that their principal purpose is not lobbying, and that therefore, they do not have to register. The National Association of Manufacturers, for example, for years claimed that it was a multipurpose organization and therefore did not have to register, that influencing legislation was not its principal purpose. Many organizations claim that such confusion over what the law means entitles them not to file. Though it is tempting to lay blame on groups who obviously engage in lobbying but do not register, the law *is* vague and thus enforcement is impossible.

In 1954, the Lobbying Act was debated before the Supreme Court in the case of *U.S.* vs. *Harriss.* Serious questions about the act's constitutionality were raised—after all, the First Amendment guarantees everyone the right to ask for favors from legislators. The Court ruled that the Lobbying Act was constitutional and that Congress could compel the disclosure of lobbying activities.

But unfortunately, the ruling created further confusion and even more loopholes. It specified that the disclosure requirement could be applied only when the lobbying method was *direct* communication with Congress. Thus a major lobbying technique—grass roots lobbying—was exempted from the provisions of the law. The Court did specify that an *artificially stimulated* letter writing campaign was included in its definition of direct pressure. But the fact is that if a lobbying group stirs up 6,000 letters, this can easily be viewed as "indirect" pressure. If the letters are sent by a group whose "principal purpose" is not lobbying, the group is exempt. In effect, grass roots lobbying is still not covered by this law. Groups like the NRA simply ask members to "voice their views." Who can prove that the resulting letter was prompted by an "artificial" letter campaign? It's impossible.

Chief Justice Earl Warren wrote in his majority opinion that the law only wants to know who is being hired, who is putting up the money, and how much. But the fact is that we often still don't know who, how much, or what for because the law is so vaguely worded.

A further gaping hole in the law is that it leaves it up to the individual lobbyist to decide what portion of actual lobbying expenditures he or she will report. Some groups are known as big spenders, but this doesn't necessarily mean they actually spend more on lobbying. They may simply interpret the law more strictly than others; they may report everything that could even remotely be considered as spending for lobbying. What happens is often ludicrous. One lobbyist who worked for an amendment to a trade law reported twenty-four dollars in expenses for the quarter (a three-month period) and no salary. The reason: the principal purpose of his salary was not payment for lobbying. Therefore, he did not have to report salary.

Another lobbyist said, "My association would pay my salary if I never went near Congress, and therefore I refrain from reporting any of my salary as received for lobbying." A lobbyist for one of the nation's best-known professional organizations reported a total salary of $194 and total expenses of fifty cents in a recent quarter. During this period, the organization was engaged in a massive lobbying effort against a major bill.

On the other hand, the chief lobbyist for the AFL–CIO reported $18,700 in salary in a recent year and $1,769 in lobbying expenses. A woman who represents a peace group reported total receipts for one reporting period of more than $64,000 and lobbying expenses of over $20,000. But five lobbyists for one of America's largest corporations reported a total salary of $6,107 and $730 in expenses—for all five of them! At that time they were engaged in a successful lobbying campaign of great importance to their company.[10]

The law should not let the lobbyist decide what proportion of his or her lobbying expenses to report—the way is left too clear for evasion of the reporting requirements, and without more accurate reporting, citizens do not know how much is being spent to influence government.

Another problem is that the Lobbying Act of 1946 does not cover lobbying done before the executive branch of the federal government. This is a loophole that should be corrected if there is to be a new law. And the law does not cover lobbying of Congress that is done *by* executive branch aides. If reporting requirements are tightened for other kinds of lobbyists, executive branch staff members should also be included. Finally, there is no agency empowered to enforce the lobbying law. So even if its definitions were clear as crystal, there wouldn't be anyone to haul in offenders.

RECOMMENDATIONS

The Lobbying Act of 1946 has been evaluated by Congress on several occasions, but so far no bill that would regulate lobbying directly has cleared both Houses. Several lobby disclosure bills are now pending. Any new lobby law should include these provisions:

1. Define a lobbyist as any individual who is paid to influence legislation and who devotes any portion of his or her time to these efforts. In other words, the phrase "principal purpose" would be stricken from the law.

2. Reports should be filed by lobbyists on a quarterly basis

with a federal agency set up to police and enforce the law. These reports should list lobbyists' salaries, expenditures, and the names, addresses, and purpose of those who furnish the money; they should list all money spent for the purpose of influencing legislation, regardless of the amount.

3. Lobbyists should be able to make political contributions as long as they are recorded in the quarterly reports.

4. Indirect grass roots lobbying campaigns should be reported. Such a report could include letter and telegram campaigns, advertising, books, pamphlets, salaries of executives, lawyers and publicists, and operating budgets. But if a company advertises in national magazines that promote a general point of view—ads that urge people to support "free enterprise" or "free trade"—but that don't relate to a specific bill before Congress, those ads should not fall under our definition of grass roots lobbying.

5. Any new law should apply to lobbying by the executive branch, as well as lobbying by private interest groups before the federal regulatory agencies and the executive departments.

Suggestions have been made that lobbyists should keep records of their contacts. These entries would include the person contacted and what was discussed. The report would be available to the public. This kind of restriction would probably be unenforceable and should not be included in any new lobby law.[11]

IMPROVING THE SYSTEM

As our government is now structured, lobbies are essential. Lobbyists formally represent the desires of thousands of Americans by focusing on specific interests persistently and thoroughly. They act as communications agents for these messages. They monitor government activities so the interests of their members

Bribery, corruption... I hope the system lasts until we're in charge.

are protected. Lobbyists today speak for thousands of constituents who feel they otherwise do not have a voice in Washington, the state legislature, or the city council room. The current system could be improved, however, if lobbying were more strictly regulated.

FOOTNOTES

Chapter One

1. Lewis Anthony Dexter, *How Organizations Are Represented in Washington* (Indianapolis and New York: Bobbs-Merrill Co., 1969), p. 5.
2. James Deakin, *The Lobbyists* (Washington, D.C.: Public Affairs Press, 1966), p. 54.
3. Ibid., p. 55.
4. Ibid., pp. 55–56.
5. Karl Schriftgiesser, *The Lobbyists* (Boston: Little, Brown & Co., 1951), quoted in Deakin, p. 57.
6. Deakin, *The Lobbyists*, p. 58.
7. Ibid., pp. 58–60.
8. Ibid., pp. 73–74.
9. Fred J. Cook, *Lobbying in American Politics* (New York: Franklin Watts, Inc., 1976), p. 80.

Chapter Two

1. Emmanuel Celler, "Pressure Groups in Congress" in H.R. Mahood, *Pressure Groups in American Politics* (New York: Scribner's, 1967), pp. 233-34.
2. Lester Milbrath, *The Washington Lobbyists* (Chicago: Rand McNally, 1963), p. 233.
3. Ibid., p. 233.
4. Ibid., pp. 211-12.
5. Ibid., pp. 220-26.
6. Ibid., p. 222.
7. Ibid., p. 225.
8. Ibid., p. 226.
9. Mark J. Green, James M. Fallows, and David R. Zwick, *Who Runs Congress?* Ralph Nader Congress Project (New York: Bantam Books, 1972), p. 41.
10. Milbrath, *The Washington Lobbyists*, p. 168.
11. Material on Coastal States Gas taken from Paul Burka, "Power Politics," *Texas Monthly*, May 1975, pp. 68-97.
12. Milbrath, *The Washington Lobbyists*, p. 113.
13. Ibid., p. 124.
14. Ibid., p. 125.
15. Ibid., pp. 127-28.
16. Ibid., p. 129.
17. Ibid., p. 129.
18. Ibid., p. 137.

Chapter Three

1. Deakin, *The Lobbyists*, pp. 202-03.
2. Ibid., p. 203.
3. Robert J. Kukla, *Gun Control* (Harrisburg, Pa.: Stackpole Books, 1973), p. 87.
4. *American Rifleman*, vol. 123, no. 6, June 1975, p. 8.
5. Kukla, *Gun Control*, p. 79.
6. *American Rifleman*, vol. 123, no. 6, June 1975, p. 43.
7. Deakin, *The Lobbyists*, p. 207.

8. "Shootings, Mail, Lobbying Push Congress to Act," *1968 Congressional Quarterly Almanac* (Washington, D.C.), p. 563.
9. Deakin, *The Lobbyists*, p. 211.
10. "No Action Taken To Regulate Firearms Shipments," *1964 Congressional Quarterly Almanac* (Washington, D.C.), p. 272.
11. Kukla, *Gun Control*, p. 21.
12. U.S., Congress, Senate, Committee of the Judiciary, *Hearings Before the Subcommittee to Investigate Juvenile Delinquency*, March 1968, p. 439.
13. Dan David, "Gun Control—Lobbying Activities of the National Rifle Association," 1970, unpublished paper, pp. 9–10.
14. *New York Times*, June 16, 1968, Sec. IV, p. 17.
15. *1968 Congressional Quarterly Almanac*, p. 564.

Chapter Four

1. Cook, *Lobbying in American Politics*, p. 114ff.
2. John Gardner, *In Common Cause* (New York: W. W. Norton & Co., Inc., 1972), p. 81.
3. Elizabeth Drew, "Common Cause: Conversation with a Citizen," *The New Yorker*, July 23, 1973, p. 35.
4. Louise Sweeney, "John Gardner of Common Cause," *Christian Science Monitor*, February 20, 1974, Sec. 2, F 1.
5. Common Cause, *Action Manual*, p. 22.
6. *Action Manual*, pp. 18–19.
7. Joan Libman, "Californians Are Divided by Plan for Policing Elections, Lobbying, and Conflicts of Interest," *Wall Street Journal*, May 31, 1974, p. 32.

Chapter Five

1. Milbrath, *The Washington Lobbyists*, p. 352.
2. Congressional Quarterly Service, *Legislators and the Lobbyists* (Washington, D.C., 1965), p. 17.
3. Milbrath, *The Washington Lobbyists*, p. 343.
4. Ibid., pp. 343–44.
5. Ibid., pp. 297–98.

6. Green, Fallows, and Zwick, *Who Runs Congress?*, pp. 27–28.
7. Ibid., pp. 6–13.
8. "New CC Data Underscores Need for Public Financing," *In Common: The CC Report from Washington,* vol. 5, no. 6, June 1975, p. 5.
9. "Campaign Law Decision," *Congressional Quarterly,* January 31, 1976, p. 253.
10. Deakin, *The Lobbyists,* pp. 224–38.
11. Some of these suggestions come from Deakin, *The Lobbyists,* pp. 267–70.

BIBLIOGRAPHY

* Carney, John P. *Nation of Change: The American Democratic System.* New York: Canfield Press, Harper & Row, 1972, chapter nine.

Congressional Quarterly Service. *Guide to Current American Government,* published semiannually. See also the *CQ Almanac* (annual), and the *CQ Weekly Report.*

Deakin, James. *The Lobbyists.* Washington, D.C.: Public Affairs Press, 1966.

* Dexter, Lewis Anthony. *How Organizations Are Represented in Washington.* Indianapolis and New York: Bobbs-Merrill, 1969.

* Freedman, Leonard. *Power and Politics in America.* North Scituate, Mass.: Duxbury Press, 1974, chapter five.

* Green, Mark J., Fallows, James M., and Zwick, David R. *Who Runs Congress?* Ralph Nader Congress Project. New York: Bantam Books, 1972.

Mahood, H. R. *Pressure Groups in American Politics.* New York: Charles Scribner's Son's, 1967.

McConnell, Grant. *Private Power and American Democracy.* New York: Alfred A. Knopf, 1966.

* Indicates books more suitable for younger readers.

Milbrath, Lester. *The Washington Lobbyists*. Chicago: Rand McNally, 1963.

Rossiter, Clinton, ed. *The Federalist Papers*. New York: New American Library of World Literature, 1964.

INDEX

Alaska, 6
Alaska Federation of Natives, 6
Alaska Public Interest Coalition, 6
Alaskan pipeline, 6
Alyeska Pipeline Service Company, 6
American Association of Retired Persons, 4
American Bar Association, 47
American Camping Association, 4
American Cancer Society, 59
American Civil Liberties Union (ACLU), 74, 91
American Federation of Labor-Congress of Industrial Organizations (AFL-CIO), 7, 72
American Gas Association, 6
American Nurses Association, Inc., 7
American Petroleum Institute, 6
American Postal Workers Union, 7
American Rifleman, The, 43–44
American Society of Composers, Authors, and Publishers, 4

American Trucking Association, Inc., 7
Antelope Airlines, 4
Anti-Saloon League, 17
Arco Fuel Oil Company Inc., 6

Black, Hugo, 18
Bribery, 81, 83
Buchanan, James, 15
Busing, 6

Campaign contributions, 6, 30, 83–84, 86–92
Campaign finance laws, 90–92
Campaign financing, 6
Celler, Emanuel, 22
Center for the Study of Responsive Law, 58
Church, William C., 42
Citizen Research Foundation, 87
Coastal States Gas, 33–35
Coca-Cola Company, 4

Collaboration, 26
Commitment, 35–36
Common Cause, 4, 6, 7, 27, 29, 63–64, 66–67, 69–72, 74–75
Condon, Frederick Hughes, 57
Congress, structure of, 92–93
Cross-lobbying, 29, 46–47, 71
Curtis, Thomas, 80

Dairy scandal of 1971, 83–84, 86–87
Daniel, Frank C., 46
Deakin, James, 15
Declaration of Independence, 11–12
Directory of Registered Lobbyists and Lobbyist Legislation, 4
Disabled American Veterans, 7
Distilled Spirits Institute, 4
Diven, A. S., 16
Dodd, Thomas, 41, 48
Dodd bill, 41, 44, 47–49
Douglas, Paul, 30–31
Drew, Elizabeth, 64

Eighteenth Amendment to the Constitution, 17
Emergency Committee for Gun Control, 52, 53
Entertainment, 30–31
Exxon Corporation, 6

Federal Communications Commission (FCC), 8
Federal Election Campaign Act of 1971, 30, 90
Federal Election Campaign Act of 1974, 30, 90–91
Federal Election Campaign Act Amendments of 1976, 30, 92
Federal Election Commission, 91, 92
Federal Firearms Act of 1934, 41
Federal Regulation of Lobbying Act of 1946, 7, 18, 93–97
Federalist Papers (Jay, Madison, and Hamilton), 13
Fields, Andrew C., 16

First Amendment to the Constitution, 3, 12, 95
First Continental Congress, 12
Foreign Agents Registration Act of 1938, 8
Foreign governments, lobbying by, 3, 8–9

Gardner, John, 62–64
Gas Supply Committee, 7
General Motors (GM) Corporation, 56–58
Georgia, 12
Glassen, Harold, 50–51
Glenn, John, Jr., 52
Grass roots lobbying, 27, 29, 70–71, 75, 82, 95–96, 98
Gun control, 41–53, 75
Gun Control (Robert Kukla), 42, 49
Gun Control Act of 1968, 53

Hamilton, Alexander, 13
Hardin, Clifford, 84

Interest groups, 4, 21, 24
International Association of Chiefs of Police, 47
Interstate Commerce Commission (ICC), 7, 8, 58

Japanese-American Citizens League, 4
Jay, John, 13
Jefferson, Thomas, 13
Job satisfaction, 36–37
Johnson, Lyndon B., 48–49, 51

Kennedy, John F., 41
Kennedy, Robert F., 49, 51, 52, 53
King, Martin Luther, Jr., 49, 51, 53
Kukla, Robert, 42, 44, 49

Legislative Reorganization Act of 1946, 18, 93

Life insurance companies, 16
List, Friedrich, 14
Lobbying
  campaign contributions, 6, 30, 83–84, 86–92
  Common Cause, 4, 6, 7, 27, 29, 63–64, 66–67, 69–72, 74–75
  as communication, 22
  comprehensive strategy, 32
  cross-lobbying, 29, 46–47, 71
  definition of, 2, 22
  early, 12–14
  entertainment, 30–31
  example of, 2–3
  by foreign governments, 3, 8–9
  grass roots, 27, 29, 70–71, 75, 82, 95–96, 98
  history of, 11–12
  indirect methods, 29–32
  National Rifle Association, 22–24, 27, 29, 42–53, 59, 75
  nineteenth century, 14–16
  President's lobby, 10–11, 79–80
  private, 4–6, 75
  public interest, 4–6, 59–63, 74–75
  by reform groups, 16–17
  regulation, 18, 78–99
  scope of, 6–8
  state and local, 3, 33–35
  voting records, publicizing, 30
  See also Lobbyists
Lobbying Act of 1946, 7, 18, 93–97
Lobbyists
  characteristics of job, 22–24
  commitment of, 35–36
  effectiveness of, 78–83
  job satisfaction, 36–37
  Nader, Ralph, 56–58, 62
  registration, 4, 18, 93–94
  as representatives, 20–22
  services provided by, 24–27
  sucessful tactics, 27–29
  See also Lobbying
Lobbyists, The, (Deakin), 5
Local lobbying, 3, 33–35

Madison, James, 13
Middle East relations, 6
Milbrath, Lester, 22, 26, 27, 32, 35, 79–82
Mobil Oil Corporation, 6

Nader, Ralph, 56–58, 62
Nader's Raiders, 58
National Association for Advancement of Colored People (NAACP), 59
National Association of Manufacturers (NAM), 7, 95
National Federation of the Blind, 4
National Highway Traffic Safety Administration, 62
National Rifle Association (NRA), 22–24, 27, 29, 42–53, 59, 75
National Shooting Sports Foundation, 29, 47
National Student Association–Government and You, 4
National Traffic and Motor Vehicle Safety Act of 1966, 58, 62
National Wildlife Federation, 6, 29 47
Nixon, Richard M., 6, 10, 78, 86, 87
No-fault insurance, 6

Omnibus Crime Bill, 49, 51
Oswald, Lee Harvey, 41

Perot, H. Ross, 89
Powell, William, 86
President's lobby, 10–11, 79–80
Private interest, 4–5, 75
Prohibition, 17
Proposition Nine, 72, 74–75, 78
Public interest, 4–6, 59–63, 74–75

Recce, Susan, 22–24, 33, 53
Reform groups, lobbying by, 16–17
Registration of lobbyists, 4, 18, 93–94
Regulation of lobbying, 18, 78–99

Republican Governor's Conference, 51
Research, 24–25
Ribicoff, Abraham, 57
Roche, James, 58
Roosevelt, Franklin D., 10
Rummel, Bartlett, 48

Second Amendment to the Constitution, 42, 49
Seniority system, 92–93
Sierra Club, 6, 59
South Korea, 8–9
Southwestern Peanut Shellers Association, 4
State lobbying, 3, 33–35

Temperance Movement, 17
Testimony at hearings, 25
Texas Railroad Commission, 34
Traffic safety, 6, 57, 60, 62
Traffic Safety Act of 1966, 58, 62
Trout Unlimited, 6
Tydings, Joseph D., 52

United Auto Workers, 6, 7
U.S. Cane Sugar Refiners' Association, 4
U.S. Conference of Mayors, 51
U.S. vs. Harriss (1954), 95
U.S. Savings and Loan League, 7
Unsafe at Any Speed (Nader), 56–57
Urban Coalition, 63

Vietnam War, 6
Voting records, publicizing, 30

Warren, Earl, 96
Washington Lobbyists, The (Milbrath), 22, 26, 27, 32, 35, 79, 81, 82
Watergate scandals, 78
Weed, Thurlow, 15–16
Wheeler, Wayne Bidwell, 17
Wildlife Management Institute, 47
Williams, Harold, 74
Wyatt, Oscar, 33–35

ABOUT THE AUTHOR

Karen Sagstetter, a native of Houston, Texas, has an M.A. degree in English from Rice University and an M.A.H. degree in creative writing from the State University of New York at Buffalo. She has in the past taught high school as well as written articles for various education magazines.

Currently Ms. Sagstetter is teaching creative writing part-time, writing, and working as a research coordinator for the Bureau of Education for the Handicapped in Washington, D.C.